GRACE
REVEALED

The ultimate measure of Christianity (or any religion) should be whether it helps human beings live meaningful lives—even in the face of tragedy. In *Grace Revealed*, Fred Sievert has collected nineteen stories of humans from a wide spectrum of society and Christian traditions who have discovered the transforming grace of God in crises. These stories remind us that God's grace is not principally a theological construct or a lofty sermon, but the reality of God in our lives—a reality that helps us live meaningfully, even when we have been devastated by life.

—GREGORY E. STERLING, the Reverend Henry L. Slack
Dean and the Lillian Claus Professor of New Testament,
Yale Divinity School

Fred's mission is clear—to spend the rest of his life telling people about God's grace. In this book, *Grace Revealed*, Fred shares people's stories of suffering, addiction, abuse, and loss, which prove to be the ultimate opportunity for God to display His incredible gift of mercy and redemption. These stories will inspire you to look at your own life and see just how powerful God's grace really is!

—KEVIN PALAU, president, Luis Palau Association; author of
Unlikely: Setting Aside Our Differences to Live out the Gospel

Much hope can be found in the amazing stories of the Bible, but they happened so long ago that it can be difficult to relate to the circumstances and people. God has not stopped creating amazing stories in the lives of those who cry out to Him, but the stories are rarely shared and even more rarely shared in an accessible style and format that can bring hope, healing, and transformation to people in crisis today. *Grace Revealed* does exactly that. With insightful background on today's struggles, thoughtful reflections, and helpful biblical references, Sievert weaves these amazing contemporary stories of God's grace into an uplifting and easy-to-read tapestry of hope, healing, and transformation for those struggling with life's toughest challenges.

—PAUL MICHALSKI, founder, Integrous LLC; president, NCS New Canaan (founding chapter of the New Canaan Society)

In Sievert's book, grace is not a theological concept or a religious term. Grace is the mode of God's presence as experienced and expressed by flesh-and-blood people; it is a reality pulsating with life, bearing as many faces as there are human lives and situations and taking on as many forms as there are sufferings and delights, defeats, and victories. In *Grace Revealed*, you will hear many grateful voices giving their best to sing their ode to grace.

—MIROSLAV VOLF, Henry B. Wright Professor of Theology, Yale Divinity School; founder and director, Yale Center for Faith and Culture

It is common in recommending a new publication to refer to the book as a real "page-turner," suggesting that once begun, the reader will not be able to put it down. But because I loved the narratives in *Grace Revealed*, I occasionally had to put it down. The stories were as painful as they were personal, the revelations as raw as they were revealing. I came to care about these people, and my caring demanded not only my attention but my time. As a pastor, I am in the "grace business," believing that good things really do happen when people cry out for it and accept it. I can picture them singing the words of an old Christian hymn, "I love to tell the story; It did so much for me." Because it did. And with Fred's help, these men and women in crisis have now told their inspiring stories.

—WILLIAM A RITTER, pastor emeritus, First United Methodist Church, Birmingham, Michigan

Fred Sievert has made the biblical concepts of grace, forgiveness, and healing come vividly alive through these real-life experiences of people and their journeys from confusion, pain, and despair to hope, joy, and new life. One cannot come away from *Grace Revealed* untouched by the way God individually and creatively works in people's lives. Fred's ability to incorporate Scripture, commentary, and the opportunity for personal reflection will leave readers feeling both challenged and inspired to find ways in which God's grace touches them. This book will offer encouragement not only to those of deep faith, but, more importantly, to those who question God's love and ability to intervene.

—REV. REBECCA MINCIELI, senior pastor,
John Wesley United Methodist Church,
Falmouth, Massachusetts

Are you stumbling under a burden of grief, anxiety, or guilt and wondering if you dare hope in the gospel's promise that "nothing will be impossible with God"? Fred Sievert's inspiring new book will introduce you to scores of folks who have faced crises like yours and found again and again that "you cannot fall farther than God can catch you." Are you puzzling over strangely beautiful but ambiguous intimations of consolation and hope and wondering whether to trust these as whispers of God's assurance or to dismiss them as meaningless daydreams? As you read the testimonies collected here, you'll find yourself whispering, "Gosh, that's just what happened to me!" again and again. This work will be a gift to youth leaders, and group leaders will find this book a wonderful conversation starter for gatherings of all ages. Faithful Christians will value this book as a source of daily devotionals. Spiritual seekers will be deeply grateful for the guidance and company of fellow pilgrims on the way.

—SKIP MASBACK, founder and director, Yale Youth Ministry
Institute; associate director, Yale Center for Faith and Culture

Once again, Fred Sievert shows us how to take the most defining choices of Christianity seriously. These stories and discussions of strong episodes of ego, forgiveness, redemption, and love trace the arc of authentic seeking. Guidance from biblical sources, psychology, and theology deepens the analysis further.

—LAURA NASH, PhD, former faculty member, Harvard Business School and Harvard Divinity School; author of *Believers in Business* and coauthor of *Just Enough: Tools for Lasting Success in Work and Life*

Fred Sievert has hit another home run! Grace is God's unmerited favor, and each of these miraculous stories outlined in *Grace Revealed* is shining proof of this. With God, "anything is possible."

—JACK KRASULA, president of Trustinus, LLC; host of *Anything Is Possible* on News/Talk 760 WJR

This book is a treasure of stirring stories of personal crisis and Christian transformation. Each person's voice is unique yet universal—any open-hearted person will find himself or herself in these stories. The book is beautifully structured for group or personal study: smartly organized around common crises, clear questions for group and personal reflection, and suggested Scripture for memorization. I especially recommend this book for those who are self-conscious or even critical of talking about the reality of God in daily life. Talking about God's activity in one's life—testimony—is not "weird" or "self-involved." Rather, it is a crucial dimension of real faith. This book shows how testimony honors God, strengthens those in crisis, and helps others—including us, the readers.

—JOANNE M. SWENSON, ThD, senior minister, Church in the Forest, Greater Pebble Beach, California; founding minister, 12: A Foundation for Small Group Ministry

Fred Sievert is on a mission to demonstrate the grace, mercy, and power of God, and he does a masterful job in this second book of his. I found it thoughtful, emotional, inspiring, motivating, educational, informative, theologically and biblically sound, and presenting enlightening research. *Grace Revealed* is a powerful and memorable book to which many will relate, providing sound advice to those in pain, who "hurt," are helping those who "hurt," or want to understand a way to help. When I finished, I sat quietly in awe of the message, what people have endured, and how, with God's help, they turned their lives around.

—STEVEN DARTER, president, People Management SMD; author of *Lessons from Life: Four Keys to Living with More Meaning, Purpose, and Success* and *Managing Yourself, Managing Others: Learn How to Improve Effectiveness, Productivity, and Work Satisfaction*

Grace Revealed is far more than a theoretical discussion of Grace—it is a workbook for everyone who experiences pain, addiction, fear, or resentment. In other words, it is vitally relevant to each of us. Fred Sievert combines a pastor's knowledge of the Bible with real-world trauma to see how grace heals and restores fallen spirits, whether by their own action or abuse from others. It is a message of hope and love—the pure love of Christ. Read it to be inspired. Read it to find grace in your own life.

—JERRY BORROWMAN, best-selling author of sixteen biography and historical fiction books

We are all playing the game of "You Bet Your Life." You can believe what you like, but you must accept the consequences. In *Grace Revealed*, after years of misfortune and pain, men and women write about how they came to bet their lives on Jesus. Their stories are both amazing and transformative.

—PETER G. HAWKINS, investment advisor

GRACE REVEALED

Finding God's Strength in Any Crisis

FRED SIEVERT

BroadStreet
PUBLISHING

BroadStreet Publishing® Group, LLC
Racine, Wisconsin, USA
BroadStreetPublishing.com

Grace Revealed: Finding God's Strength in Any Crisis

Copyright © 2018 Fred Sievert

ISBN-13: 978-1-4245-5638-0 (softcover)
ISBN-13: 978-1-4245-5639-7 (e-book)

Unless noted otherwise, all Scripture quotations are from the Holy Bible, New International Version®, NIV® Copyright ©1973, 1978, 1984, 2011 by Biblica, Inc.® Used by permission. All rights reserved worldwide. Scriptures marked KJV are taken from the King James Version (KJV), public domain.

Stock or custom editions of BroadStreet Publishing titles may be purchased in bulk for educational, business, ministry, fundraising, or sales promotional use. For information, please email info@broadstreetpublishing.com.

Cover design by Chris Garborg at garborgdesign.com
Typesetting by Katherine Lloyd at theDESKonline.com
Author photos by Lisa Mancuso-Horn

Printed in the United States of America

18 19 20 21 22 5 4 3 2 1

This book is dedicated to my family: my wife, Sue, and my five children, Heidi, Dena, Denise, Zachary, and Cornell. Each of them has unselfishly endured my type A personality and intense working lifestyle for all too many years. Nonetheless, they have remained supportive and understanding throughout my working lifetime, and now during my post-retirement years, because they recognize that I am pursuing a divine calling—to write and speak about my faith. I love each of them dearly and will be eternally grateful for their encouragement and love.

An Important
Disclaimer

Neither the author nor the contributing writers of this book are medical professionals. Nothing written in this book, either in the research regarding the prevalence of certain physical or emotional issues or in the stories themselves, is meant to provide professional medical advice. I present medical information and statistics only to inform readers of the prevalence of certain conditions within the population.

In writing about God's healing power and loving grace, I in no way wish to diminish the importance of sound medical advice and treatment from appropriate medical professionals.

I also want to acknowledge that I am not an ordained minister. I am simply a retired corporate executive who has known the Lord for most of my life and who decided to retire early to attend divinity school to enhance my spiritual education and development. Little did I know at the time that my writing would become a ministry that reaches out to thousands of individuals who can benefit from a deeper relationship with Jesus Christ. I now view my long business career as nothing more than a mere prologue to what I am doing today—writing and speaking about my faith.

TABLE OF CONTENTS

PREFACE

Throughout my lifetime, hearing or reading about the faith journeys of thousands of Christians has substantiated my belief that individuals most often come to know Christ when they cry out to Him in a crisis. And often, their faith is reinforced, or even inspired, by the testimony of others who are willing to share the stories of their own personal relationships with Christ and how they were triggered.

This book couples those two very common elements of the Christian experience with yet a third element—the overwhelming tendency of those who come to develop a personal relationship with Christ to return God's grace in the form of Christian service to others in need.

The Christian experience many times progresses through the following three phases:

1. Experiencing a crisis
2. Receiving grace
3. Returning grace to others

Most of the inspiring and compelling stories in this book reflect all three of the above phases. These are stories of individuals who were in a crisis, either of their own volition or imposed on them by others or by external influences.

Whatever their crisis—an addiction, a serious health issue, the pain of an abusive relationship, the loss of a loved one—they all cried out to God for help. In chapter 1, I elaborate on the three ways in which people can receive the grace alluded to in phase two above.

In their desperate appeal for relief, their prayers were answered, and they were blessed immeasurably by the loving grace of God. And in their gratitude, they felt compelled to share their stories and return God's grace to others experiencing crises similar to their own.

I believe strongly in the power of spiritual sharing. In my post-retirement, post-divinity school "ministry," I have felt called to touch individuals in crisis with the stories and testimonies of those who have found relief and joy in a way that only faith in Christ and a relationship with Him can provide.

If you find yourself in a desperate crisis that is causing you great emotional pain and suffering, it is my fervent prayer that reading how others experienced God's grace can provide you with relief and a transformation that inspires you to return that grace to others in need.

AS WE BEGIN

Are you ready—and open—to experience and understand God's amazing grace in a deeper, more personal way than you ever have before?

Has life worn you down?

Are you weary of remembering past mistakes?

Have you been kicked in the teeth by illness? By the mistakes of others? By being an occupant of this planet?

Are you in crisis?

Then this book is for you.

By way of background, my thirty-year career in the insurance business now seems like nothing more than a prologue to my current endeavors and ministry. Nothing in my life has made as big a difference as living under the grace of God.

After retiring from my position as president of New York Life Insurance Company, I spent four years in divinity school and subsequently wrote my first book, *God Revealed: Revisit Your Past to Enrich Your Future.*

Since publishing that book in 2014, I have been deeply moved and spiritually enriched by the people I've met and the stories I've heard relating to God's saving grace in their lives, often in the face of life-threatening crises.

I faced a number of crises in my own life that are recounted in my first book, but *Grace Revealed* is not about me.

Instead, it features the stories of those people I've met who confided in me about the transformative power of Jesus Christ in their lives at a time of personal crisis or despair. Many suffered from addictions or personal tragedies that endangered their very existence.

Through social media and in traveling the country to make appearances related to my first book, I heard from hundreds of readers about their own encounters with God, their realization of God's grace, and their resulting commitments to serve the Lord. Those stories deeply affected me and inspired this book.

Grace Revealed was written for you.

The souls who shared their stories with me were all transformed by grace into redeemed individuals with lives empowered and guided by the loving grace of God. Hearing their stories further enlightened, inspired, and transformed me.

Whatever your personal situation may be, no matter how dire or helpless it may seem, I believe the stories in this book will touch you with the transforming power of God's grace in a way you may never before have experienced.

That is what *Grace Revealed* will do for you.

The personal stories in this book are compelling because they demonstrate how close people's lives can come to being destroyed without a realization of God's grace. They also are compelling because all the individuals recounting their stories in this book have committed to serving the Lord as a result of realizing His grace. They want to pass along God's most precious gift to others.

Even those who wish to remain anonymous in the retelling of their stories have found it cathartic to recount their examples of God's grace, and they consider it a blessing to be able to reach others who may be suffering with similar experiences or circumstances. It was God's grace that drove them into service, empowered them, and guided them. They have allowed me to tell their stories because they truly believe their realization of God's grace will help you.

In the chapters that follow, you'll read true stories of people who recovered from debilitating illnesses, addictions, and trauma through God's grace—when nothing else seemed to help them.

You'll read how each of them, in their own way, reached out to the Lord for relief. You will see how people of all ages moved from despair to an understanding of the dark places they were in to a new mind-set that made them open to realizing God's grace and accepting this gift for which Jesus Christ paid the ultimate price.

The following are just some of the people who have shared their stories of triumph in this book:

1. A woman who suffered abuse at age six by a family member, witnessed her father beating her mother, began drinking in the sixth grade, and found God in her forties. She is now an active church member who ministers to others so that, as she says, "they can experience the same healing, hope, and peace that I have received through Jesus Christ."

2. A corporate executive who served nine months in a prison camp for fraud and then turned his life over to the Lord via urging from his guardian angel, a woman he had known years earlier who had died. He now lectures to others about his transformative experience and current service to other Christians.

3. An award-winning triathlete who overcame breast cancer in 2008, as well as bulimia, and has since competed in the World Triathlon Grand Final in Mexico. She has written several books and is a frequent lecturer and contributor to Christian radio and television shows.

4. A successful corporate attorney who couldn't cope with the pressure and burden of his workload and found the Lord when his emotional state hit a dangerous low point. He left his position as a highly successful attorney to attend divinity school, become ordained, and has been a pastor of one of the largest churches in Connecticut for nineteen years. His passion now is to enhance youth ministry throughout the United States and beyond.

7. A woman who spent most of 2009 flying back and forth to Colorado to be with her twenty-nine-year-old son, who had inoperable cancer, while dealing with the weekly

emergencies of her elderly father's declining health. After losing both of them, she now speaks before various groups and teaches on the subject of coping with family illness and loss.

8. A father whose son is serving time in prison on drug charges. He now makes presentations to groups about how to recognize and cope with drug addiction in children.

9. A Vietnam veteran who was diagnosed with PTSD after returning from his tour of duty, forever haunted by the carnage he witnessed. He has established a nonprofit organization through which he helps other war veterans heal.

At that moment when a person realizes and accepts God's grace, his or her life is transformed forever and will never be the same.

Regardless of the crisis you may be facing, God's grace can heal you and give you hope for a happier, more fulfilling future while mending the debilitating wounds of the past. The stories in this book are about individuals who realized and accepted God's marvelous gift of grace, and how they, out of love and gratitude, are returning that same love and grace to countless others through an enduring commitment to a life of Christian service.

The stories of real people have always moved me most of all. Stories about the empowering nature of God's grace throughout all of life's mistakes and drama have not only shown me the bigness of God; they also have empowered me to live with more grace—for myself and others.

As you read this book, may God's loving grace bring you through your personal crisis in a way that richly blesses you—and encourages you to share your story and His blessings with others.

GOD'S GRACE— A BLESSED GIFT

N
o book on grace could start with anything else but the Bible's
message of grace, which becomes astonishingly up front and
clear once you recognize how the focal point of the Bible—Jesus
Christ—truly is the source of all grace that comes from the Creator.

God's free and unmerited gift of grace embodied in the birth, life,
death, burial, and resurrection of Jesus Christ has emboldened, nour-
ished, and sustained millions of Christians throughout history and
continues to do so today. Receiving God's grace is not the culmination
of your Christian experience but, rather, the potential commencement
of a lifetime of Christian faith and service. It enables you to overcome
any crisis and transforms and empowers you under the guidance of the
Holy Spirit to return God's marvelous gift to others.

The following verses encapsulate the overarching theme of this
book:

Grace was foreshadowed in the Old Testament: "We all, like
sheep, have gone astray, each of us has turned to our own way; and
the Lord has laid on him the inequity of us all" (Isaiah 53:6).

Grace is granted for unfailing faith in Jesus Christ: "With great
power the apostles continued to testify to the resurrection of the Lord
Jesus. And God's grace was so powerfully at work in them all" (Acts
4:33).

Jesus declares His grace to be sufficient: "But he said to me, 'My grace is sufficient for you, for my power is made perfect in weakness'" (2 Corinthians 12:9).

Grace, once realized, is transformative: "Do not conform to the pattern of this world, but be transformed by the renewing of your mind" (Romans 12:2).

And grace precedes good works, not vice versa: "And God is able to bless you abundantly, so that in all things at all times, having all that you need, you will abound in every good work" (2 Corinthians 9:8).

The inspiring stories shared in this book are compelling testimonies to the modern-day veracity of these ancient Scriptures. All these stories give accounts of people in desperate need—men and women in crisis—who realize God's grace and, in response, are transformed and called to a life of enduring Christian service, empowered and guided by God's greatest gift—grace.

Merriam-Webster defines *grace* biblically. It is described as "unmerited divine assistance given humans for their regeneration or sanctification." The word *unmerited* emphasizes that we receive what we do not deserve. A blog post on Christianity.com notes that "mercy, not merit," is shorthand for grace. The author writes the following:

> Grace is most needed and best understood in the midst of sin, suffering, and brokenness. We live in a world of earning, deserving, and merit, and these result in judgment. That is why everyone wants and needs grace. ... Grace is the opposite of karma, which is all about getting what you deserve. Grace is getting what you don't deserve and *not* getting what you do deserve. Christianity teaches that what we deserve is death with no hope of resurrection.[1]

Before you can accept God's grace, you have to realize it is intended for you. When you realize God's grace, you take the first step toward accepting that unconditional gift that is yours, regardless of how much you think you do or do not deserve it.

San Antonio preacher and best-selling Christian author Max

Lucado says, "God's grace is not a gentle shower washing away the problem. It is a raging, roaring river whose current knocks you off your feet and carries you into the presence of God."[2] Those who tell their powerful stories of redemption in this book can certainly attest to that.

How do we often come to realize God's grace? Through faith—by believing in Christ and His power to heal our lives.

Three Types of Grace

As you read the stories in this book, you may find that they raise interesting theological questions about the nature and timing of God's grace. These questions have also intrigued me over the years as I've compared my experience with those of others who have become Christians and experienced God's loving grace at different moments in their own faith formation.

In my studies, I have found John Wesley's beliefs about grace to be instructive. They allow me to reconcile my personal experience with the differing experiences of some of my Christian friends.

John and Charles Wesley were the founders of the Methodist movement within the Anglican Church in England during the eighteenth century. This movement emphasized works of piety (working with the Holy Spirit to grow in personal relationship with God) and works of mercy (working with the Holy Spirit to help others grow in relationship with God by addressing their spiritual and physical needs). The doctrines and beliefs that came from John and Charles through this movement became the Wesleyan Doctrines of the United Methodist Church.[3]

Based on John Wesley's belief that grace affects us in primarily three different ways, contemporary Wesleyan theology recognizes three distinct types of grace that the *United Methodist Book of Discipline* summarizes as follows:

1. **Prevenient grace**—"We acknowledge God's prevenient grace, the divine love that surrounds all humanity and precedes all of our conscious impulses. This grace prompts our

first wish to please God, our first glimmer of understanding concerning God's will, and our 'first slight transient conviction' of having sinned against God."[4]

My own experience and those of many of the contributors to this book were examples of prevenient grace from God before a deep personal relationship with Christ existed.

2. **Justifying grace** (justification and assurance)—"We believe God reaches out to the repentant believer in justifying grace with accepting and pardoning love. Wesleyan theology stresses that a decisive change in the human heart can and does occur under the prompting of grace and the guidance of the Holy Spirit."[5]

In many of the stories in this book, God poured out His grace after the person in crisis had already been saved and had a personal relationship with Christ.

3. **Sanctifying grace** (sanctification and perfection)—"We hold that the wonder of God's acceptance and pardon does not end God's saving work, which continues to nurture our growth in grace. Through the power of the Holy Spirit, we are enabled to increase in the knowledge and love of God and in love for our neighbor. New birth is the first step in this process of sanctification."[6]

In virtually all the stories in this book, those who were touched by God's grace returned that grace in Christian service to others in need.

The Most Powerful Weapon against Adversity

The poetic wisdom of Isaiah is not only comforting and reassuring but also foreshadows the grace that can come through our faith in Jesus Christ:

Do not fear, for I have redeemed you; I have summoned you by name; you are mine. When you pass through the waters, I will be with you; and when you pass through the rivers, they will not sweep over you. When you walk through the fire, you will not be burned; the flames will not set you ablaze. For I am the LORD your God, the Holy One of Israel, your Savior. (Isaiah 43:1–3)

The apostle Paul, in his second letter to the Corinthians, expressed his faith in the face of extreme adversity: "We are hard pressed on every side, but not crushed; perplexed, but not in despair; persecuted, but not abandoned; struck down, but not destroyed" (2 Corinthians 4:8–9).

The author of Hebrews upholds Jesus Christ as a model for how we should approach the throne of God in anticipation of grace: "For we do not have a high priest who is unable to empathize with our weaknesses, but we have one who has been tempted in every way, just as we are—yet he did not sin. Let us then approach God's throne of grace with confidence, so that we may receive mercy and find grace to help us in our time of need" (Hebrews 4:15–16).

The true stories in this book will reinforce your faith and better prepare you to realize and accept God's loving, unmerited gift of grace. They will demonstrate the varying ways in which so many individuals have realized God's grace (either through prevenient grace or through justifying grace by reaching out to their savior Jesus Christ in earnest prayers of supplication) and how sanctifying grace led to a subsequent commitment to Christian service to others.

Precisely defining what grace is and how to achieve it is difficult at best. The Scriptures noted earlier and the views of reliable theologians, authors, and clergy help us understand its essence. Grace typically manifests itself in undeniable ways as God's intervention in our lives, providing us with relief from our struggles or crises. Grace is real, and our understanding of it is individualized and experiential. The stories in this book are concrete examples that collectively help us more fully understand the nature of God's grace and the ways in which real people have experienced its miraculous benefits.

Jesus Paid the Ultimate Price

Grace became more accessible with God's sacrifice and the passion of Jesus Christ: "For God so loved the world that he gave his one and only Son, that whoever believes in him shall not perish but have eternal life" (John 3:16). And as the apostle Paul says, "But because of his great love for us, God, who is rich in mercy, made us alive with Christ even when we were dead in transgressions—it is by grace you have been saved" (Ephesians 2:4–5).

God's grace takes many forms and is available to sinners and saints alike. The Bible tells us that humans are naturally inclined to sin, and that, in fact, "all have sinned and fall short of the glory of God" (Romans 3:23).

Perhaps the best biblical example of a sinner who foreshadowed Christ's role in future grace is that of the criminal on the cross next to Jesus, who through the grace of Christ was guaranteed a spot in paradise. The criminal symbolically personified dozens of generations of future sinners who would experience the Lord's saving grace:

> One of the criminals who hung there hurled insults at him:
> "Aren't you the Messiah? Save yourself and us!" But the other
> criminal rebuked him. "Don't you fear God," he said, "since
> you are under the same sentence? We are punished justly,
> for we are getting what our deeds deserve. But this man has
> done nothing wrong." Then he said, "Jesus, remember me
> when you come into your kingdom." Jesus answered him,
> "Truly I tell you, today you will be with me in paradise."
> (Luke 23:39–43)

Each of us is like the second criminal. No matter what we have done in the past, we have access to God's unmerited grace. We don't deserve to be freed of the consequences of our sins. But Jesus Christ has made that sacrifice for us, just as He did for the self-confessed criminal with whom He was executed.

Pastor Rick Warren reminds us that God's grace is completely free to us, but Jesus paid His life for it:

> That's why it is only through Jesus that we can find the grace of God—because He's the one who paid for the grace we receive. ... Because you receive the grace of God through Christ alone, the Lord doesn't look at you like you think He does. God's Word says those of us who have accepted God's grace are 'in Christ.' That phrase is used more than 120 times in the Bible. To be 'in Christ' means that when God looks at you, He doesn't see all your sins, failures, and rough spots. When you're 'in Christ,' God just sees Jesus. You may see the scars, the mess, and the problems, but God sees perfection in Christ.[7]

So why would God give us grace at such a high cost? Because God is love, and that love is unconditional and unbounded. He wants to use us to further His kingdom. He wants us to reflect His love in our relationships and our interactions with others: "Dear friends, let us love one another, for love comes from God. Everyone who loves has been born of God and knows God. Whoever does not love does not know God, because God is love" (1 John 4:7–8).

Warren also emphasizes the importance of gratitude and obedience: "So in light of what Jesus has done for us, how should we respond? We must be grateful. One way we can show our gratitude to God is by making our lives count. You can't really understand the grace of God and the price He paid to make it available to you while living how you want to live, ignoring the commands of Jesus, or wasting your life on things that don't matter."[8] As the apostle Paul put it, "You were bought at a price. Therefore honor God with your bodies" (1 Corinthians 6:20).

You will see in these true stories about individuals whose lives God has transformed that His lavish gift of grace is so powerful that every one of them is now serving Him. They all desperately cried out to God, realized His grace, accepted it, and are showing others how He can change their lives as well.

Empowered and Guided by God's Marvelous Gift

Grace is a gift from God, but it is not something we can accept passively. Quite the contrary—realizing and accepting God's grace often drives us to make a conscious decision out of deep gratitude and love to abandon sin and live the kind of life He has chosen for us. Once He offers grace to us, we are empowered and guided by our miraculous transformation to respond by sharing our experience and our knowledge of grace with others. Grace does not affect us passively; it empowers and guides us to follow God's example as we navigate life's hills and valleys:

> For the grace of God has appeared that offers salvation to all people. (Titus 2:11)

> For sin shall no longer be your master, because you are not under the law, but under grace. (Romans 6:14)

Grace strengthens us as well, arming us with the conviction and confidence to overcome old ways of being and thinking and enabling us to be transformed: "Be strong in the grace that is in Christ Jesus" (2 Timothy 2:1).

Biblical Lives Transformed by Grace

The Bible tells several stories of how the disciples and other individuals were transformed by God's grace and were empowered and guided into lifelong Christian service.

Perhaps the most powerful and compelling such story is that of Saul, the self-righteous Pharisee and persecutor of Christians who encountered Jesus on the road to Damascus (read Acts 9:1–31) and was forever transformed into a follower of Christ. Thereafter he was known as the apostle Paul, and he wrote as many as thirteen books of the New Testament.

Zacchaeus, a dishonest tax collector, was one of the last people Jesus met before His death. Jesus surprised many bystanders by calling Zacchaeus down from a sycamore tree and going to the house of this sinner as a guest (read Luke 19:1–10).

Zacchaeus' transformation as a result of this encounter was to give half of his wealth to the poor and to return fourfold the taxes he had cheated from others.

In the twenty-first century, examples of the marvelous grace of God are numerous and varied. It is difficult to articulate a common cause or template that describes the form or source of realized grace. The stories in this book, however, present very clear and compelling examples of God's unmerited grace in its many manifestations in the lives of Christians and among those seekers who turned to Christ in their desperation.

I trust that you will be inspired and blessed as you read these modern-day stories of men and women who experienced God's grace in their time of crisis and were transformed forever by those divine experiences.

Healing Insights

- The three types of grace (prevenient, justifying, and sanctifying) described by John Wesley can help us understand the varying ways in which people receive grace and are affected by it.

- God's grace transforms us and empowers us under the guidance of the Holy Spirit.

- God's grace is completely free to us, but Jesus paid His life for it. He gives us the gift of grace because He wants to use us to further His kingdom.

- Grace does not affect us passively, and we do not accept it passively. Rather, it empowers and guides us to follow God's example as we navigate life's hills and valleys. It also compels us to pay that grace forward to others in Christian service.

2

CONFRONTING PHYSICAL, SEXUAL, OR EMOTIONAL ABUSE

I t is difficult to understand how one of the wealthiest and most socially advanced countries in the world is the breeding ground for all types of abuse, from childhood sexual abuse to spousal abuse and elder abuse.

The effects of abuse can last a lifetime and wreak havoc on a survivor's mental, emotional, and physical health.

For example, one study of 57,000 women in 2013 found that those who experienced physical or sexual abuse as children were twice as likely to have eating disorders than those who were not abused. A 2015 *Atlantic* article documenting the prevalence of obesity in childhood sexual assault survivors explained that there is some evidence that stress induces the body to store fat—"a vestige of a time in human evolution when this would have been useful." The article goes on to describe other health consequences often caused by sexual abuse:

> Chronic stress also triggers the release of chemicals called pro-inflammatory cytokines, which prevent insulin from being taken up by the muscle cells. This is called insulin resistance, and it's strongly correlated with obesity. ... Also,

among women who were hospitalized for psychiatric treatment after bariatric surgery to induce weight loss, one study found that 73 percent had a history of childhood sexual abuse.[1]

Sexual abuse is one of the most common and damaging types of abuse a person can endure.

Alarming Statistics about Sexual Abuse

America has more than 42 million survivors of sexual abuse. It is estimated that between 66 and 90 percent of sexual-abuse victims never tell anyone they were abused. In 90 percent of all child sexual abuse cases, the perpetrator is someone the child knows, loves, or trusts.[2]

Given the tragic ways abuse affects people later in their lives, it is not surprising that people who have been abused are much more likely to land in jail or prison. According to the American Society for the Positive Care of Children, people who experience child abuse and neglect are about nine times more likely to become involved in criminal activity. And 14 percent of men in prison and 36 percent of women in prison in the United States were abused as children. This is about twice the frequency seen in the general population.[3]

According to Adults Surviving Child Abuse, child abuse has many potential effects later in children's lives, and some of them are severe. Children naturally rely on their parents and other caregivers for safety, security, love, understanding, nurturance, and support. When an adult violates that trust, the betrayal can impair the child's ability to form attachments throughout life. People who were abused as children often suffer job disappointments, frequent relocations, failed relationships, and financial setbacks.

Emotional problems that people who were abused often experience later in life include the inability to regulate emotions like rage and terror; negative self-perception; chronic feelings of isolation, despair, and hopelessness; and intense suicidal feelings.

Childhood abuse can manifest as physical symptoms later in life too. Commonly reported health concerns that result from child abuse include depression, anxiety disorders, addictions, personality disorders, eating disorders, and sexual disorders.[4]

A common theme throughout this book is the fact that the difficulties people experience at one life stage can impact the problems they face in later life stages. Many organizations are working tirelessly to prevent neglect and abuse and to treat the survivors. But there is one remedy that seems to work consistently—God's grace.

Below are Bible verses that can provide comfort to survivors of abuse and insight to people who have abused others:

Bible Verses for Survivors of Abuse

The LORD is a refuge for the oppressed, a stronghold in times of trouble. (Psalm 9:9)

May the God of hope fill you with all joy and peace as you trust in him, so that you may overflow with hope by the power of the Holy Spirit. (Romans 15:13)

Do not be anxious about anything, but in every situation, by prayer and petition, with thanksgiving, present your requests to God. (Philippians 4:6)

The LORD is close to the brokenhearted and saves those who are crushed in spirit. (Psalm 34:18)

And the God of all grace, who called you to his eternal glory in Christ, after you have suffered a little while, will himself restore you and make you strong, firm and steadfast. (1 Peter 5:10)

You will not fear the terror of night, nor the arrow that flies by day, nor the pestilence that stalks in the darkness, nor the plague that destroys at midday. (Psalm 91:5–6)

For if you forgive other people when they sin against you, your heavenly Father will also forgive you. But if you do not forgive others their sins, your Father will not forgive your sins. (Matthew 6:14–15)

But to you who are listening I say: Love your enemies, do good to those who hate you, bless those who curse you, pray for those who mistreat you. (Luke 6:27–28)

Bible Verses for Those Who Have Abused Others

Do not conform to the pattern of this world, but be transformed by the renewing of your mind. Then you will be able to test and approve what God's will is—his good, pleasing and perfect will. (Romans 12:2)

If anyone causes one of these little ones—those who believe in me—to stumble, it would be better for them to have a large millstone hung around their neck and to be drowned in the depths of the sea. (Matthew 18:6)

Therefore, if anyone is in Christ, the new creation has come: The old has gone, the new is here! (2 Corinthians 5:17)

Children should be embraced, blessed, and nurtured. God loves children, and those who harm and abuse them are inviting God's wrath. The Lord's love for children was clearly depicted in the gospel of Mark, when the disciples tried to prevent children from coming to Jesus.

People were bringing little children to Jesus for him to place his hands on them, but the disciples rebuked them. When Jesus saw this, he was indignant. He said to them, "Let the little children come to me, and do not hinder them, for the kingdom of God belongs to such as these. Truly I tell you, anyone who will not receive the kingdom of God like a little child will never enter it." And he took the children in his arms, placed his hands on them and blessed them. (Mark 10:13–16)

My prayer is that every child would grow up in a loving, nurturing home with Jesus Christ as the central focus. In far too many homes today, belief in Jesus is not a child-rearing necessity.

Here are some true stories that demonstrate the various ways abuse can ruin lives and that also serve as examples of how God's grace can transform the lives of abusers and survivors.

Conquering the Cage of Guilt

Mary DeMuth is a Christian blogger, international speaker, and the author of more than thirty books. She has survived many hardships dating back to her early years. Here is an overview, in her words, about how God has helped her heal from the pain of childhood sexual abuse.

Mary DeMuth

I grew up in a world where I didn't feel safe. Sexual abuse at age five, three divorces, the death of my father, drug abuse permeating my childhood neighborhood—many of these traumas I kept quiet. For years I lived under the unwritten, unspoken mandate that to tell was to betray.

Healing Erupts in the Light of Truth

It wasn't until I met Jesus at fifteen that the secrets started to spill. Knowing Jesus and His extravagant love for me helped me know that no matter what I shared, I was still wildly adored by Him. He gave me the courage to tell my story and an insatiable desire to be whole. Throughout college, where friends dared to pray me toward healing, I learned that healing erupts in the light of truth. Simply put, if we hide things, we fester. But if we want Jesus to uncage us, we have to tell the truth.

It does hurt when we acknowledge the pain from the past. Thankfully, Jesus comes to our rescue in two ways.

Consider Peter's words in 1 Peter 2:24: "'He himself bore our sins' in his body on the cross, so that we might die to sins and live to righteousness; 'by his wounds you have been healed.'" See the beautiful juxtaposition there? Jesus' death and sacrifice means He not only bears our sin, but His outrageous act also heals the wounds we receive from others.

I am living testimony that it's possible to heal from trauma. It's possible for Jesus to so dynamically transform you that others would never know you walked that path of pain.

God Transforms Broken Lives

My life affirms this kind of personal revolution. I was nothing—a girl who questioned her worth—yet God chose me to show how well He can transform a broken life. The apostle Paul wrote, "But God chose the foolish things of the world to shame the wise; God chose the weak things of the world to shame the strong" (1 Corinthians 1:27).

When I became a Christian, though, I didn't quite understand all of this. I thought I was supposed to be strong and perfect. I thought that for others to see Jesus in me, I had to push down my pain and not share it openly. I had to play-act my way toward perfection.

I now realize that God takes us on quests, not day hikes. Healing takes time. Throughout my twenties, when I married and had children, old wounds reemerged. As a sexual abuse victim, I found the marriage bed scary. And when my daughters reached the age I'd been when neighborhood boys raped me (five years old), I panicked. For a long time, I disconnected from my three children and husband because the risk of intimacy was just too great.

In my thirties, I met with a couple of counselors. I moved across the country, which helped me heal from festering memories. I finally realized that Jesus loved me just for me. I still had questions about all the whys of my past, but I also felt contentment for the first time.

Think of Your Past as a Stage Where God Can Display His Power

You may be thinking, "Yes, but you don't know what I've endured. You don't see the aftermath of my pain." You're right. I don't. But I'd like to invite you to think differently for a moment. Instead of seeing the past as a detriment, begin to see it as a stage for God to display His power. You actually have an advantage. Why? Because you know your need for Jesus. You know you can't heal on your own. Your weakness is the very starting place for Jesus to let you out of your cage.

That's the beauty of weakness. That's why I can thank God for the fear, pain, and shame of my childhood. Because all those things helped me see my extreme need for Jesus to set me free.

You have a choice. You can either move forward or wallow in the past. Oswald Chambers wrote, "Let the past sleep, but let it sleep on the bosom of Christ, and go out into the irresistible future with Him." We have an irresistible future ahead of us. After we've told the truth about the past and experienced God's healing, it's time to cultivate a holy anticipation for what God will unfold.

I am happy to say today that I'm a joyful mother of three adult children, the wife of twenty-seven years to my husband, Patrick, and a full-time writer. I have the uncanny privilege of writing and speaking about Jesus' ability to restore our lives.

I used to think joy was impossible for me. But now I walk in it every day. That's my prayer for you too.

Mary shares the following verses on her website, www.marydemuth. com, to encourage those who are struggling to overcome the lasting effects of sexual abuse:

Therefore, if anyone is in Christ, the new creation has come: The old has gone, the new is here! (2 Corinthians 5:17)

Brothers and sisters, I do not consider myself yet to have taken hold of it. But one thing I do: Forgetting what is behind and straining toward what is ahead, I press on toward the goal to win the prize for which God has called me heavenward in Christ Jesus. (Philippians 3:13–14)

My Thoughts on Mary's Story

Mary has an inspiring way of seeing the good in situations that, on the surface, seem to be anything but good. She says to those who have experienced abuse, "You actually have an advantage. Why? Because you know your need for Jesus. You know you can't heal on your own." Her ability to see strength in vulnerability is a testament to her strong faith in God.

Also, Mary reminds us that Jesus' painful death on the cross heals the wounds we receive from others. Jesus experienced unspeakable suffering, and He has compassion for our suffering. We can learn from Mary's example that we need to acknowledge our pain and turn it over to Jesus so that He can "uncage" us from our pain.

Time for Personal Reflection

1. Initially, Mary feared disclosing her abuse and harbored the painful shame and guilt for a long time. She even moved away from her physical surroundings to remove herself from an environment that constantly reminded her of the past. If you have ever suffered from abuse, what was your initial way of coping?

2. Mary's faith in Jesus Christ led to her relief and freedom from guilt and shame. Do you continue to hold onto your pain instead of giving it to God?

3. Only you can determine if you'll choose Mary's path to recovery by revealing your experience to a trusted friend

or counselor or decide, as others have, that it just can't be disclosed at this point in your life. Whichever approach you take, know that you can open up to the One who has given His life for you. He will eliminate your pain and return you to a healthy, guilt-free, and shame-free existence. Lay your burden at the feet of Jesus Christ and believe that He will open a path to full recovery. Ask for His healing and loving grace in persistent prayer. I encourage you to stand on His promises and expect a miracle. And, like Mary, when you are ready, you may be empowered to impact the lives of other survivors by sharing your story with them.

Amazing Grace

The next story is about intra-familial sexual abuse. "Rita" is a sixty-nine-year-old woman whose brother-in-law abused her sexually when she was only ten years old. She wishes to remain anonymous.

Rita did not tell anyone about the abuse until thirty years later, and she always struggled to understand the meaning of love. Through those years, God put people in Rita's path to lead her to peace, contentment, and healing. Thirty years after the abuse happened, bolstered by God's grace, she told her abuser that she forgave him.

Here is her story.

I was born in the Northeast and have lived within the same twenty-mile radius my entire life, although I have traveled extensively. I am single and have no children, but I have many nieces and nephews, whom I helped raise.

I was baptized in the Methodist Church and attended until age ten, when my family left the church. My father had a disagreement with the pastor. As a teenager, I attended an Episcopal church and was confirmed at the age of seventeen. I knew God existed but always felt unworthy of His love and grace.

I had three siblings: a brother who is seventeen years older than me, a sister who is fifteen years older, and a brother who is three years older than I am. My older brother and sister both got married when I was five years old, and I became an aunt at the age of six. Both my brother-in-law and my sister-in-law became part of our family, and I loved both of them as siblings. To this day, I am very close to my sister-in-law.

What My Mother Told Me

When I was ten, my brother-in-law started sexually abusing me. The abuse lasted for years. This was during the same time our family left the Methodist Church. For many years, I thought God was punishing me for leaving the church. I was a shy introvert, and the abuse caused me to withdraw within myself. As a result, I had a miserable childhood. I was confused, afraid, bitter, ashamed, hurt, resentful, and angry.

My mother and sister found out about the abuse somehow. I did not tell them, so I don't know how they found out. I remember standing in the kitchen, and they were so angry. My mother told me it was my fault. I couldn't believe she was telling me I had caused it to happen! I was ashamed and in tears, and I really didn't know what was going on.

The abuse was devastating to me and affected me emotionally and in my interpersonal relationships. I managed to function and work—not only to support myself, but to help raise five of my sister's six children when she divorced her husband (the abuser).

My father never knew about the abuse. Even so, it really damaged my relationship with him because I blamed him for not protecting me at the time. He died at the age of sixty-seven, when I was twenty-six. I didn't realize until years later that he didn't know anything about it, so he could not have protected me.

My mother died at the age of eighty-eight, when I was fifty-one. She had a lot of medical problems. It was expected that I would always be there to take care of her, and I was. That made me even angrier, but I kept it inside.

Family Events and My Abuser

As long as my mother was alive, I had to go to family affairs. My sister divorced my brother-in-law, the abuser, and he was estranged from the family for several years. He remarried and lived in the South. After his second wife divorced him, he returned to the area and was invited to various family functions again. It was a difficult time for me because he was always around. Because of his alcoholism, he almost died of a bleeding ulcer. After his recovery, he married a third time.

My mother died in 1998. At her gravesite, the abuser put his hands on my arm, and he wanted to hug me. I pushed him away and rushed off. I may have even hollered—cried out—I can't remember. It was too emotional. His adult granddaughter, who I am very close to, stopped me and wanted to know what was going on. I said, "Keep your grandfather away from me." Eventually I told her what had happened. She said she had often wondered why she was never allowed to be alone with him. At that point, I knew they must have known something.

I later learned that he had also molested his oldest daughter. I have never spoken with her about it. We almost discussed it at one point, but I guess it was just too difficult to bring out into the open. He had four daughters, and I would not be surprised if he abused the others too.

That day at my mother's gravesite was when I made the decision, "I am not going to speak to him. My mother is dead now. I don't have to do this now." If he was around, I was not going to be around. As a result, I missed a lot of family functions.

Forgiveness at a Funeral

This went on until my sister died eleven years later, in 2009, at the age of seventy-nine. I was sixty-two. She had COPD and emphysema from sixty years of smoking. She had Alzheimer's disease too. She was cremated, and of course her ex-husband, the abuser, was invited to the memorial service. I remember standing there, watching him come through the door. He was seventy-seven years old at that point and in poor health, and it was hard for him to walk.

I remember thinking, "I'm glad to see him suffer a little bit." At the service, I gave a eulogy. He was sitting right in the front row, and of course I didn't look at him. When I sat down, we sang the closing hymn, "Amazing Grace." I listened to the words, and this powerful message came to me from God: "If you cannot forgive your brother-in-law of his sin, how can I forgive you of your sins?" I still resisted forgiving him, but God was working on me.

At the gathering after the service, I finally walked over and said, "You know who I am?"

He said, "Yes, I do, Rita." Then I said the three words that began my healing process after fifty years: "I forgive you." I added, "Do you understand what I'm saying?"

He said, "Yes, I do. Thank you." He never said, "I'm sorry," but he did thank me. He wanted to touch my hand, but I pulled away and said, "That's it. Good-bye."

It was a huge relief for me! I felt the weight of all those decades of shame, confusion, anger, hatred, revenge, and sadness just lift up from me. I felt truly free for the first time since I was a little girl.

Sustaining Grace

I didn't realize it at the time, but God placed people in my life to help me cope and continue on my faith journey. My seventh-grade homeroom teacher read a Bible verse, and we prayed the Lord's Prayer each morning. The Lord's Prayer was allowed in school back in the fifties. My eighth-grade math teacher was an inspiration to me and led me on the road to becoming an accountant. Both teachers were Christians and active in their churches.

These are just a few of the people God placed in my path to help me in this long struggle to let go and forgive not only my abuser but my family. His love and grace have sustained me, even though I did not recognize His gifts.

Helping Others through Pain

When I was thirty-eight, my close friend, Mary, introduced me to Jesus. I knew God was there before that, but I really didn't know Jesus at that point. I returned to the Methodist Church and am still an active member. I serve on the Missions Committee and was the chairperson for three years. I am a trustee, and I serve on the Finance Committee and the Altar Guild. I have served on several mission trips locally and in Africa.

It wasn't until 1987, when I was forty years old, that I told anyone about the childhood sexual abuse. I told the pastor of my church, and that was the beginning of my journey of healing. That same year, I attended a Southern New England Emmaus three-day spiritual retreat over a long weekend. The purpose of the retreat was to walk closely with God. I really learned a lot about Him and myself, so that was another turning point for me. I felt God's grace surrounding me. I realized that He had been with me all along.

I have shared my story through the Emmaus community. It is difficult for me to tell others what happened because it's so personal, but I see that it helps people who have been through similar experiences. A few months ago, during a weekend retreat, there were some people there who had suffered abuse as children. And on other mission trips there were a few people on my team with whom I shared my story. They told me that hearing what I went through helped them deal with their own situations.

The Reality of God's Love

My latest struggle came to light this past Lenten season as our church studied living prayer. Over several months, our pastor preached on love: "Love others as you would love yourself." I have always struggled with the word "love." I knew God loved me, but I did not love or forgive myself. So how could I love anyone else? And what is this word called "love"? When I was being abused, my abuser would tell me he "loved" me. My question through the years was "So what is love?" Is love like the love my abuser showed, or is love a word that means abuse? I know God is real, but I have always questioned why He allows children to be abused by their family members or others.

My answer to this love problem came through prayer and counseling by my current pastor. Very early one Sunday morning during my prayer time, I witnessed a bright light and the warmth of God's love surrounding me. It was a love beyond any human understanding, and my God healed all the guilt, shame, anger, resentment, fear, and hurt. John 3:16 finally became real. With God's grace and counseling from my pastor, I finally have forgiven myself and love myself just as I am. I am finally at peace.

My prayer for anyone reading this story is that you may find the same love and peace that I found through prayer with our heavenly Father and His son, Jesus Christ.

These three verses are among my favorite verses. They have given me strength and comfort over the years.

For God so loved the world that he gave his one and only Son, that whoever believes in him shall not perish but have eternal life. (John 3:16)

But those who hope in the LORD will renew their strength. They will soar on wings like eagles; they will run and not grow weary, they will walk and not be faint. (Isaiah 40:31)

The LORD is my shepherd, I lack nothing. He makes me lie down in green pastures, he leads me beside quiet waters, he refreshes my soul. He guides me along the right paths for his name's sake. Even though I walk through the darkest valley, I will fear no evil, for you are with me; your rod and your staff, they comfort me. You prepare a table before me in the presence of my enemies. You anoint my head with oil; my cup overflows. Surely your goodness and love will follow me all the days of my life, and I will dwell in the house of the LORD forever. (Psalm 23:1–6)

My Thoughts on Rita's Story

It baffles me that so many parents disbelieve their children who reveal to them that they have been sexually abused. The abuse is horrific enough, but to have a parent—in Rita's case, her mother—tell the child the abuse is her own fault, that adds another dimension of confusion, hurt, anger, guilt, and shame to the child who is already suffering. It's no wonder that it took Rita decades to begin the healing process.

I find it remarkable that Rita also spent much of her time, energy, money, and emotional resources helping raise five of her sister's six children when her sister divorced her husband, the abuser. Rita was able to focus on the welfare of her nieces and nephews and not allow her horrific experiences keep her from caring for them.

Rita also showed tremendous courage and faith in God when she confronted her abuser in a calm, confident, but firm manner decades after the abuse happened. I can't imagine how difficult that must have been.

Time for Personal Reflection

1. Is there someone you need to forgive for something he or she did to you? Do you feel that it is necessary to tell the person "I forgive you" to his or her face, or is it enough to simply forgive the person and move on? Genuinely forgiving is the key to freeing yourself from the chains of unforgiveness, whether or not you tell the person you have done so.

2. Remember that forgiving is not the same as condoning the person's actions. Recognize that forgiving the other person does not mean you think what happened is OK; it just

means you are letting God take control of the situation, and you are no longer condemning the person for what he or she did to you.

3. Do you find yourself ruminating on what happened, even after you have decided to forgive a person? It might make you feel morally superior to the other person, and that may keep you from looking into your own heart. If this is happening to you, ask the Lord to help you truly forgive. Ask others to pray for and with you; ask God to bring permanent forgiveness into your heart.

You're Never Alone

Teresa Rosenthal

According to the Rape, Abuse & Incest National Network, or RAINN, among the cases of child sexual abuse reported to law enforcement, 93 percent of the perpetrators are someone the children know. Of those, 34 percent are family members, 59 percent are acquaintances, and 7 percent are strangers.[5] So it is more likely that those who abuse children sexually are someone the children know and trust but are not family members. Regardless of who the perpetrator is, however, sexual abuse has lifelong consequences for the survivor.

The next story is about Teresa Rosenthal, who lives in Bald Knob, Arkansas, a small town of about three thousand people. It is sometimes described as the place "where the Ozarks meet the Delta." When Teresa was a young girl, she witnessed her father's physical abuse of her mother, and it affected her deeply. Adding to Teresa's trauma was the fact that when she was only six, a family friend sexually abused her. She didn't tell anyone about the abuse for forty years, and during that time, alcohol and drug abuse, as well as anger, took their toll on her life. But God began placing people in Teresa's life to guide her to the Lord. And then, after she was saved, He began putting people in Teresa's path who desperately needed the healing that could come from her willingness to share her own story of God's grace with them.

When I was six years old, I was abused by a family friend several times. I will refer to him as "James," but that is not his real name. His family and mine had grown up together, and he would babysit for my parents. I had other brothers and sisters, and I was the youngest of the girls. He would always find a way to distract the others and then say I was being bad, so I had to go to bed. Each time the abuse happened, he would tell me it was because I was being bad and that if I told my mother, she wouldn't love me anymore. My father's moods changed radically and for no apparent reason, and James used that to keep me silent. He said that if I told my father, he would not believe me, and then I would be in more trouble for lying.

My father was physically abusive to my mother, and his moods changed often. With us kids, he would be loving and having fun one minute, and then the next minute we would be getting spanked. Most times it was way too hard and long. It was like walking on eggshells around him. I never knew what mood he was going to be in or when the violence would erupt. Sometimes my father would beat my mother and then bring her into the bedroom to show us her beaten body and say, "This is what happens when you don't listen to me."

One night, James was babysitting, and he abused me again. My mother knew something was not right with me, so she asked me if something had happened. I lied to her and told her no because I believed all the lies James had told me over and over. My mother knew I wasn't telling the truth. She and my father got into a fight that night about it, and again he beat her up. I remember sneaking into their bedroom that night and putting an icepack on her eye. I wanted to tell her I was sorry and tell her the truth, but I was too scared. After that night, James was no longer allowed in our house or around me.

I shut all that up inside me and didn't speak of it for four decades. I felt crushed for lying to my mother, and I was angry at my father and the man who abused me. I felt cheated out of my childhood. I felt ashamed of the abuse and very depressed. I was so confused. I tried to rationalize in my mind what I had done wrong to deserve it.

Alcohol Flowed Freely

When I was in the fifth grade, my father was killed in an explosion at work. I loved my father very much, and I was very sad when he died, but along with sadness, I felt both relief and anger. I felt relieved because there would be no more violence and fits of rage. I had a lot of anger in me toward my dad because I couldn't tell him about the sexual abuse and make it stop. I was angry with him for beating my mother all those times.

My mother bought a bar about a year later. She was still grieving my father's death. She still loved him, even after all she had been through, and she began to drink heavily. Our garage was stocked with boxes of alcohol for the bar. My depression and jumbled feelings grew, and I had easy access to alcohol, so I began drinking when I was in the sixth grade. My alcohol abuse—and later, drug abuse—continued for four decades, just like my anger and hurt.

At school, I became the protector of children who were being bullied. When I would see a bully picking on another kid, it would just set me off. All those feelings of anger and hurt would run through me, and I would stop the bullying in a calm but firm way.

I never showed much emotion because I put up a wall inside me and slowly started shutting out the world. I didn't like people touching me or getting too close to me. My marriage and other relationships failed because I shut down inside. I worked hard at everything I did to fill that worthlessness and lost feeling I had inside of me. I lived my life feeling that I had no purpose. I felt lost and empty, with a lot of heartache.

When I was twenty-one, my mother died of cancer, and I felt a deep sense of loss. Nine years later, I had a twin son who died at home of SIDS at only two and a half months old. Those two losses seemed to magnify the emotional trauma I had suffered as a child. My continued use of alcohol seemed to be the only way I could numb the pain. Of course, it took more and more alcohol and harder liquor. At that point, I started cutting and hurting myself. I could not deal with or understand all the pain that was inside me. When I would physically hurt myself, I could see it and understand it, and it made me focus on that pain instead of the turmoil inside me. It became harder and harder for me to keep my emotions from showing.

I love my children very much. They are the only thing that has ever made me happy. I loved them, took care of them, and was very protective of them. I was very depressed, and many, many times, I thought about suicide. I was lost and hurt, and I felt they deserved much better. I thought they would be much happier without me, and they wouldn't have to watch me destroy myself, but I could not get past the thought of leaving them and not being there to protect them.

At forty-three, I was fired for the first time ever from my job. As I was searching for employment, I got mixed in with a group and started doing meth. They talked me into bootlegging to pay my living expenses. That took me further into drinking and drugs, and within a year and a half, I was arrested five or six times for resisting arrest because I could no longer control all that anger and hurt I had bottled up inside of me for so many years.

It was at that point that I found out my daughter was going through the same thing my mother had—being physically abused by her husband. I was trying to help her, but at the time, to her, I was the bad person. I found out about an incident between my daughter and son-in-law, and I took the matters into my own hands and went after him. I went to the house where he was and became very violent and destructive. After several police arrived and a long, drawn-out struggle, I was arrested.

My Unplanned Suicide Attempt

Between my arrest and my court appearance, my son-in-law and I continued to have heated confrontations. One day I was sitting and thinking about my upcoming jail sentence of thirty-three days, for trying to protect my daughter, and my thoughts switched to thinking about my son, who was out of town with family. At the time, I was taking medications for COPD, arthritis, depression, and pain. I went to take my daily dose of medicine and ended up taking all the pills. I didn't plan it. I just decided I couldn't take any more, and at that moment I decided I didn't want to live anymore.

I don't know how much time went by, but the pills had kicked in. A neighbor walked in my door and asked me what I was doing—for what reason, I don't know. He immediately called an ambulance. I was just sitting there, happy and smiling. He asked, "What's wrong with you?" All I could do was smile. I remember feeling so relieved and happy in that moment, knowing I was going to die soon, and it was all going to be over.

The police and ambulance arrived. I remember Officer Debbie talking to me to keep me conscious. That was the last thing I remember until I woke up in a hospital. They had pumped my stomach, and I had IVs in my veins. I became very angry that I was alive. I started crying and yelled out, "Lord, I don't know what I did that's so bad, but You won't even let me die! Why are You keeping me alive to punish me?" When I was finally released from the hospital, I had to sign a Living Will Contract and be released into my sister and brother's care. After spending a few weeks with them, I was released to return home. I felt completely hopeless and empty.

The Laundromat and Laura

Two days before I went to jail, my washing machine at home went out, so I went to a laundromat. A woman walked in as I was washing my clothes, and we said hi to one another. Then two days later, I saw her in jail; it turns out that she does jail ministry. Her name is Laura. She came to my bunk and spoke to me for a minute and asked me to meet with the other women. I received my first Bible in jail, and although I didn't really understand it, I spent almost all my time writing down what I was reading from the Bible. Every Tuesday night, Laura and a couple of other ladies would come in and minister to us. I didn't know what it was about then, but something struck my curiosity as I listened and watched them.

The day before I was to be released from jail, I was having stomach problems. It was an ulcer that blew a hole in my stomach. They had to take me from the jail into emergency surgery. I was in the hospital, hooked up to tubes and a morphine IV for pain, and I had staples holding my stomach together. And then, crazy as it sounds, I unhooked everything and walked out of the hospital and all the way home.

My First Visit to Church

When I got home, the doors were boarded up because my house had been robbed while I was in jail. So I just sat outside all night by myself until morning, not having a clear thought and feeling hopeless. For the first time ever in my life, I called on God and said, "What am I supposed to do?" At that moment, I looked beside me, and there sat the Bible from jail. I opened it, and inside was the number of a church where I could reach Laura. It just happened to be Sunday morning. I called and asked for her, and she quickly called me back. She and her husband came to visit me after the morning service.

The next Sunday, Laura picked me up and took me to church with her. I was very uncertain about it all, but I remember how amazing it was seeing the people singing and worshipping. Something was hitting my heart that I had never felt before. That very day, I felt God's love and was forever changed. I had so many questions. Laura was there to answer them, and she backed them up with the Bible.

It had been a month since I had gotten out of jail and started attending church. Our pastor had been doing a series of sermons about Joseph. At that morning's service, I didn't know why, but tears were just flowing down my face the whole time as I listened to the pastor. That evening, the pastor was going to give the ending to the series on Joseph. Something was happening to me. I wasn't going to go to the evening service, but Laura called me and said, "Don't miss the service tonight. You have to hear the end of Joseph's story." She added, "Then, if you need me to back off some—if I'm coming on too strong—I will back off," she said. "But don't miss tonight."

Uncertain what was happening to me, I very reluctantly went to the service that night, and once again, as the pastor began to speak, the tears began to flow. The story about Joseph touched me deeply. I heard how Joseph forgave his jealous brothers for selling him into slavery, and it showed me how powerful God's love and grace are. I saw how in everything Joseph was going through, and the times when it seemed there was no hope, Joseph always believed and trusted in God. I knew now what was happening: I needed that hope. I needed Jesus! Laura knew what was happening, and she led me to the altar. The pastor said the Sinner's Prayer with me, and I was saved. I immediately felt hope and a wonderful peace come over me. I felt His loving grace pour over me.

I always believed in God, but I thought He was a mean God who was punishing me. I never really knew about Jesus or what it was He did. But that day I went to church, God touched me in a mighty way. He instantly delivered me from alcohol and drugs. Then I went through emotional healing at a church called Open Arms Assembly of God in Beebe, Arkansas. Jesus did what no other being could ever do. I learned the truth, and Jesus healed me.

My children and family saw the change in me immediately. My son began attending church with me and was saved at a youth convention. He has been baptized and is now a youth sponsor at our church. My daughter and son-in-law started going to church, and both were saved and baptized. Although my daughter and son-in-law are struggling in their walk with God and in their marriage, I know it is not me who can change that for them or fix it. The one thing I can do is be in prayer and with a right heart, trusting and believing in God. As Scripture tells us, "Trust in the LORD with all your heart and lean not on your own understanding; in all your ways submit to him and he will make your paths straight" (Proverbs 3:5–6).

They have to do their own walk with God and be willing. Their children are eight, seven, four, and two. I faithfully pray and believe that God will touch them and heal my family.

God's Command to Forgive

As God was healing me, it got to the forgiveness part. I realized I needed to forgive the man who had abused me as a child. I thought, "I just can't forgive him. I might as well stop now because I'm not going to forgive him." But God puts it in your heart, and once you see things through God's eyes, it allows you to forgive. It is at that point that He sets you free.

For years I hated James for what he had done to me, leading me to believe all the lies he told me. I allowed that to control my whole life. A couple of times growing up, I ran into him at some car races, and one of the times he grabbed me and hugged me. I felt so helpless, and all types of emotions ran through me. As part of my emotional healing, I was asked to try to contact him and tell him I forgave him. Laura and I searched and tried, but we could not find him. I don't know why, but his whole family had disassociated from him. For two months, we tried, but every door was closed. So we stopped trying.

Throughout the process, I struggled with what I would say to him and how he would react, but I was willing to do it if that is what it took to move on. I believe God tested me—to see if I was willing. Although I never did get to talk to James, I prayed to God, forgiving James. I asked God to touch James, cause him to turn to Jesus for forgiveness, and fill him with the same love I have experienced. I know on that day that I forgave him from my heart because I thought differently about it all. I did my part—I forgave him—and that released me. I hope he does turn to God and asks for forgiveness.

Healing and Hope for Others

I attend an amazing spirit-filled church—Whitney Lane Family Worship Center in Kensett, Arkansas. God is doing some mighty things there, and we are seeing lots of people coming in and being saved.

I attend church regularly and help out wherever it is needed. I drive the van to pick up new people visiting our church, and I help clean the church. I also participate in our In/Out Ministry, which is a group that goes out into our community to talk to people and clean yards or do any chores they may need help with. I have also gone into the jail a few times with the Jail Ministry ladies. I have had the opportunity to witness and testify to many different people.

It is amazing how God puts people in our paths that He wants us to reach out to. God put an amazing young woman in my path who owns her own business and has a heart for giving and helping people. She is married and has a son. After a short time of knowing them, they began attending church with me and my son and now are members. God put it on my heart to start talking about my story with her. I didn't understand why, but I opened up a little at a time to her. Turns out she needed to receive that same emotional healing that I went through. She, too, has been healed, and it is amazing to see her grow in her walk with God and reach out to people. She recently gave her testimony of the healing power of Jesus and the freedom in forgiving.

Recently, I got to go on a mission trip to Belize with our church. When I got back, God kept putting it on my heart to tell my testimony to the church. The subject of childhood sexual abuse would come up often, but it's a touchy subject, so no one ever addressed it directly. People will talk about being delivered from addiction to drugs and alcohol, but nobody ever talks about sexual abuse.

I met with the pastor, and we arranged for me to give my testimony in the church. During one service, we put some chairs up on the stage, and God used me to be open about my experience. I didn't go into great detail; the pastor would ask me questions, and I would respond. But a lot of people were moved by my story. At the end, pastor had everybody bow their heads. He asked if anyone had been abused and if they were ready to give it to God. It was a small group that night of about thirty people, and six people raised their hands. The pastor and his wife met with those people. And more people from church came to me in the next few weeks to talk to me because they, too, were abused.

Beyond Deception

There are so many people who live life by what the devil has spoken to them. I was broken at six years old, and for forty years I was deceived by the devil. All I had to do was call on God, and my life was forever changed. God loves us all so much, and His desire is that not even one of us perish but have life through His Son, Jesus Christ. He will not force His love on us, but He is there with us, waiting for us to call on Him. No matter where we've been, what we've done, or what has been done to us, God will take all the bad and use it for His purpose: "And we know that in all things God works for the good of those who love him, who have been called according to his purpose" (Romans 8:28).

God has had to do a lot of healing in me. A big part of that healing happened when God showed me how to forgive. So many times, we want to put sin in categories, from small to big. God showed me sin through His eyes. James' act of sexually abusing me was the same as my abuse of drugs and alcohol. He has the same right to come to Christ for forgiveness as I did. God's Word clearly demands that we forgive others so that we, too, may be forgiven: "And when you stand praying, if you hold anything against anyone, forgive him, so that your Father in heaven may forgive you your sins" (Mark 11:25).

My freedom came when I chose to forgive James. By forgiving him, it also allowed me to forgive my father and also to forgive myself for the choices I had made in my past.

It has been an amazing journey. Some of it has not been easy because God had to totally renew my mind and heart. I would not change any of it. Each part of my journey has served to teach me and help me grow in my relationship with God. I know now how much God loves me, and I know now what Jesus did: He died so that I may have life. I know now that God does not cause all things to happen in our lives. But as His Word says, no matter what happens, if we give it to Jesus, He will take what seems very bad to us and turn it to His good for His purpose.

I am forever changed, and all it took was for me to call on God. For the first time in my life, I have peace and hope. I am now forty-nine, and I know the truth. It has set me free in a way only Jesus could do. The same God whom I thought was mean and punishing three years ago pours out much love on me, and I can't help but deepen my relationship with Him. I have no words that could explain how amazing God is to me. Jesus is my everything; I am nothing without Him. I want to live my life for Jesus, and it is my greatest heart's desire to help reach the lost and broken so that they may experience the same healing, hope, peace, and grace that I have received through Jesus Christ. To God alone be all the glory! "Not to us, LORD, not to us but to your name be the glory, because of your love and faithfulness" (Psalm 115:1).

———————

Teresa says, "The Bible is the tool God has given us as a guide for life. No matter the circumstance or where you are at in your walk with God, the Bible speaks to everyone." These are a few of the first verses she said she had to speak over and over to herself and apply as she began her walk with God:

> In my distress I called to the LORD; I cried to my God for help. From his temple he heard my voice; my cry came before him, into his ears. (Psalm 18:6)

> He heals the brokenhearted and binds up their wounds. (Psalm 147:3)

Not that I have already obtained all this, or have already arrived at my goal, but I press on to take hold of that for which Christ Jesus took hold of me. Brothers and sisters, I do not consider myself yet to have taken hold of it. But one thing I do: Forgetting what is behind and straining toward what is ahead. (Philippians 3:12–13)

I can do all this through him who gives me strength. (Philippians 4:13)

My Thoughts on Teresa's Story

Teresa has done a masterful job of articulating the pain she endured as a result of dual traumas: childhood sexual abuse and witnessing her father abusing her mother. These traumas affected Teresa for the next forty years of her life. Like many abuse survivors, she turned to alcohol, drugs, and self-harm as ways to cope with the wounds that cannot heal without God's grace.

Forgiving someone who has harmed us is difficult. Some people are never able to do so, and the inability to forgive damages them further, for the rest of their lives. Teresa said it well: "God puts it in your heart, and once you see things through God's eyes, it allows you to forgive. It is at that point that He sets you free." We all can learn this life-changing lesson that it took Teresa four decades to realize.

Teresa's story also is a testament to the way God puts people in our paths to lead us where He wants us to go. God put Laura in Teresa's life at a time when Teresa was giving up on ever feeling anything other than pain. And now, God is putting Teresa in other women's lives to provide them with comfort and godly guidance as she helps them make that difficult journey from brokenness to healing and forgiveness. Not only has Teresa been liberated from her painful past but she has also become a blessing and a conduit of the same liberation to many others. She is returning God's amazing grace.

Time for Personal Reflection

1. Teresa said, "My freedom came when I chose to forgive James. By forgiving him, it allowed me to forgive my father and also to forgive myself for the choices I had made in my past." Have you ever forgiven someone and then discovered that forgiving one person made it easier to forgive others—and yourself? If you are struggling to obey God's command to forgive others as He forgave us, know that doing so will set you free.

2. Teresa became the protector of bullied children at school. She couldn't stop the abuse she was experiencing, but she could come to the aid of other children who were being bullied. Have you experienced something similar in your own life—becoming an advocate for someone else, even though you felt you couldn't be your own advocate? What do you think it takes to make that leap to being your own advocate?

Healing Insights

- God's grace has proven to transform the lives of abusers and survivors.

- Sexual abuse affects survivors in significant ways, usually for the rest of their lives. One of the most difficult things to do is to forgive someone who has inflicted that abuse. But Matthew 6:15 says, "But if you do not forgive others their sins, your Father will not forgive your sins." Someone who has endured abuse at the hands of another will not truly heal until he or she forgives the perpetrator. This is not the same as condoning the actions, though. It simply means you are giving the situation to God and not carrying the pain and suffering around anymore.

- Although it can be difficult to find any positive consequence of abuse, it is true that a person who has survived abuse can counsel, comfort, and help other abuse survivors in a unique way. If you have experienced abuse, you can offer empathy, guidance, and hope to others who have been abused because you understand how they are feeling.

A Prayer for Those Struggling to Recover from Abuse

The stories in this chapter are about crises related to abuse. If you have ever suffered at the hands of an abuser, here is a prayer that you can modify to reflect your specific situation.

Dear heavenly Father, please heal my heart, body, and soul from the lasting damage that physical, sexual, and emotional abuse has caused. Please help me live my life without viewing all my experiences through the lens of the abuse. Wrap Your loving arms around me and comfort me. I know You are the only one who can heal my pain and let me move forward. Please restore my hope in the future and fill my heart with happiness to replace the joy that was taken from me at such a young age.

I know that the ideal outcome is that I will put this situation in Your loving hands and forgive the person who committed such vile acts against me at a time when I was young and trusting. I feel as if I am far, far away from that goal, and I pray that You will help me get there. I know I will never be truly free until I can forgive, and I need to lean on You to get there.

In Jesus' name I pray. Amen.

3

OVERCOMING ADDICTIONS

M ost of us can think of examples of friends or family members for whom alcoholism or drug abuse destroyed a marriage and seriously impacted the lives of the children in the family. The same can be said of gambling, adultery, and pornography. Emerging addictions that have surfaced in recent years like video games and cell phone texting can have equally serious consequences.

Addiction to any substance or activity eventually becomes all-consuming and renders the person powerless over its influence. Many addicts are constantly in crisis mode.

This is the American Psychological Association's (APA's) definition of addiction:

> *Addiction* is a chronic disorder with biological, psychological, social, and environmental factors influencing its development and maintenance. About half the risk for addiction is genetic. Genes affect the degree of reward that individuals experience when initially using a substance (e.g., drugs) or engaging in certain behaviors (e.g., gambling), as well as the way the body processes alcohol or other drugs. Heightened desire to re-experience use of the substance or behavior, potentially influenced by psychological (e.g., stress, history

of trauma), social (e.g., family or friends' use of a substance), and environmental factors (e.g., accessibility of a substance, low cost) can lead to regular use/exposure, with chronic use/exposure leading to brain changes.[1]

The APA definition specifically refers to drug use and gambling, but as noted above, people can become addicted to all sorts of things. Breaking free from the clutches of any addiction typically requires intervention, behavioral change, and an intrinsic desire to become free from the compulsive behavior. Calling out to the Lord for His strength, power, and grace greatly increases the chances of overcoming an addiction. The stories in this chapter powerfully attest to that fact.

Drug abuse is one of the most common types of addiction in America and represents a behavior for which a significant level of reliable data is available. The many other forms of addiction are less easily documented, but they too most certainly are increasing as the same economic and environmental factors and pressures are at work in the lives of those Americans who are susceptible to many addictive behaviors.

Illicit drug use in the United States has been increasing according to the National Institute on Drug Abuse (NIDA):

In 2013, an estimated 24.6 million Americans age twelve or older—9.4 percent of the population—had used an illicit drug in the past month. This number is up from 8.3 percent in 2002. ... Most people use drugs for the first time when they are teenagers ... Drug use is highest among people in their late teens and twenties ... Drug use is [also] increasing among people in their fifties and early sixties. This increase is, in part, due to the aging of the baby boomers, whose rates of illicit drug use have historically been higher than those of previous generations.[2]

Unfortunately, the same NIDA study demonstrates that delivering traditional recovery services to individuals struggling with addiction has proven challenging. According to their data, "there is a large 'treatment gap' in this country. In 2013, an estimated 22.7 million Americans (8.6 percent) needed treatment for a problem related to drugs or alcohol, but only about 2.5 million (0.9 percent) received treatment at a specialty facility."[3]

While both secular and Christian treatment centers can be effective, most report relatively low success rates and high relapse rates. The stories of some of the individuals highlighted in this chapter report their failure to achieve relief and permanent sobriety with professional help, even after many visits to treatment centers.

The reality is that addictions of all kinds are running rampant in today's society. They overpower men and women of all ages, ethnicities, religions, and occupations. They ultimately can control and ruin people's lives. With near certainty, I can say that most human beings are either in crisis from an addiction or know someone close to them who is.

This chapter highlights real-life stories of individuals who not only overcame their addictive behaviors but are also now thriving and helping others by the grace of God and through their personal relationship with Jesus Christ.

There are no easy cures for addiction. But there is someone standing ready to assist you. Belief in Jesus Christ and the resulting grace of God have helped thousands overcome addictive behaviors and return to happier, more normal and thriving lives free from the grip of enduring addictions.

The following are just a few of the key Bible verses that have provided strength on the journey to recovery for the many individuals who have shared with me how grace can be found in any crisis, particularly the crisis of addiction:

> Not only so, but we also glory in our sufferings, because we know that suffering produces perseverance; and perseverance, character; and character, hope. (Romans 5:3–4)

> I will strengthen you and help you; I will uphold you with my righteous right hand. (Isaiah 41:10)

The LORD is close to the brokenhearted and saves those who are crushed in spirit. (Psalm 34:18)

Therefore, if anyone is in Christ, the new creation has come: The old has gone, the new is here! All this is from God, who reconciled us to himself through Christ and gave us the ministry of reconciliation. (2 Corinthians 5:17–18)

The Riches of Grace:
From Prison to Business and Ministry

Coss Marte
(Photo by David Duncan)

Coss Marte is the founder and CEO of Con-Body, a prison-style fitness boot camp in New York City.[4] The company encourages community members to push themselves in ways they cannot imagine, both physically and emotionally.

While serving five years in prison on drug charges, Coss was transformed by reading Scripture in solitary confinement. And he made the most of his time in his nine-by-six-foot prison cell by developing a unique and effective exercise program without the need for any equipment. The resistance exercises used only his body weight. Committing himself to this program, Coss was able to lose seventy pounds in just six months. He saved his own life after prison doctors told him he was likely to live only five years because of his poor health.

He is using his life experience and skills to serve others. He has more than five thousand customers and has hired others with criminal histories. Coss is a graduate of Defy Ventures, an entrepreneurship, employment, and character-training online program for people with criminal histories.[5]

Here is Coss' story, excerpted from a TEDx Talk he presented recently.

Think for a moment: Was there a turning point for you? A point at which you took the other road? Many of us have one. Mine was when a stamp fell out of a Bible. I'll get back to that later, but first let me tell you about my road to success—how I became a kingpin.

Becoming a Teenage Drug Kingpin

At the age of nineteen, I was worth $2 million. I had access to expensive cars, I dressed in suits, and I was busy passing out my business cards. So busy, in fact, that I went through about ten thousand business cards in a couple of months. I was so busy that I needed seven phones, because my success came before the iPhone, and the flip phones could hold only fifteen hundred contacts. I was a kingpin, a highly successful drug dealer. I had a lot of people working for me, and many of those people were in their forties and fifties, answering to this twenty-something guy.

How did I get rich so fast? Well, I was motivated. I hated being poor.

My mother came to this country alone. She was six months pregnant with me. Three months later I arrived, an American citizen. It was just her and me for a while. My brother and sisters came later. My mom went to work in a factory, sewing. It was the mid to late 1980s, and at the time she was earning just a few cents per item. She would sneak me into the factory and hide me under her sewing bench. I would stay there all day—ten hours at a time—waiting for her to finish work.

We lived on the Lower East Side, and I was exposed to drugs very early. They were all around me. Not in my house, because my mom wasn't involved, but in my building. I took for granted the dope lines outside our building. I thought it was something normal to see people shooting up in the stairwells when I'd come home from elementary school. But even as an ambitious kid, I wasn't involved with it. I was out collecting bottles to return them to the bodega and make a couple dollars.

My family—we didn't have much. Basically, I just wore the same pair of corduroys to school and a dirty T-shirt. I saw these other kids with Jordan sneakers and then I'd see things on TV and say, "I want that." I hated the fact that I didn't have a game system to play with while I sat under the factory bench waiting for my mom to finish work. Poverty makes you hungry. You are driven by what you don't have—by what you want, believe me. I hated being poor. Put another way, I wanted to be rich.

As I got to be ten and eleven, I was free to roam around because basically everybody was family. My whole family lived in my building. So one of my cousins who was involved in the drug trade asked me if I wanted to smoke weed. I didn't want to, but I was curious, and I took the first step.

Then I thought, "Why not buy some and sell it?" I had worked the whole summer and had a hundred bucks saved. I bought an ounce of weed. I took that and made 300 bucks off it, and from there it just kept growing and growing. I became the weed guy. In my busiest year, I had an operation that had twenty employees and served thousands of customers using flashy cars and cell phones.

A guy in my neighborhood took me under his wing, and I was his worker on the corner of Broome and Eldridge St. When I was seventeen, he left—he moved to Pennsylvania—and he handed me his business. I basically took over the operation and the people who worked for him. I was still going to school, but I was out there day and night—I was out there on a milk crate twenty-four hours a day. My workers saw that I worked hard—worked all the time—and they respected that. But I was dealing with crackheads. Crackheads are loud; crackheads are obvious. I got arrested at age eighteen in a crack house, and I did a year. (I'd been in and out of jail since I was thirteen.)

Going High-Class

When I came out, the neighborhood was gentrifying, so I changed my target market. I stopped dealing with crackheads and started dealing with doctors, lawyers, and rich, high-class people. I had everybody who was working with me dress in suits and ties and drive expensive cars. I'd go into bars and drink and smoke with these people. I could read who was there for drugs, and I told them, "I'm running a twenty-four-hour cocaine operation. Whatever you need, whenever." I had a taxi service that would drive the drugs to a location. I was working and delivering and driving around in Lincolns and Mercedes.

Then one of my chief workers backstabbed me. He was stealing customers and product and money just disappeared. Then I didn't trust anyone. So I started managing everything myself. I took away this guy's phone so he couldn't steal from me anymore. I didn't know he'd been working with federal agents. The phone was tapped. That meant I was sending all my workers to the feds. And then I got caught with drugs and money. I went to prison.

I was on my third felony. I was being charged as a kingpin—isn't that what I was? Fat and in prison, but still a kingpin. What comes with the title is a sentence of twelve to twenty-four years. I married my son's mom at Riker's Island. He was a year old.

Prison and Fighting Death

Maybe I was in prison, but that didn't stop me. I operated my business with the phone. I even made hooch under my bed—five gallons a week—and sold five-dollar cups. I still had that demon—the drive never to be poor again. But I was facing a long prison term—no more suits, no more expensive rides.

The prison doctors examined me. And they delivered big news to me. They said I had five years to live, and I probably wouldn't live out my term because my health was so bad. Even facing a decade or more in prison, I didn't want to die. I worked out a whole series of exercises that I began doing in my nine-by-six-foot cell.

I didn't think of it at the time, because in my mind, I was still a kingpin—I was still selling. But something else was going on inside me. The exercises worked out so well that I could go on living, but it turns out that I was developing a whole new approach to life and work. These are the same exercises I use in my fitness classes today at ConBody.

After losing all the weight, I started helping other prisoners use my exercises. I helped twenty inmates lose a combined total of one thousand pounds.

I also had an opportunity to go to a boot camp. It was just like a military boot camp, and if I succeeded in the boot camp, it would lessen my sentence down to three years. I was ready. I had only three years and two months to do. And then I'd be down to two months and I'd get out of prison. But I got into an altercation with an officer. He basically beat the crap out of me. He placed me against the wall and searched me, smacking me on the back of the head. I turned around on him, and he thought I was going after him. He pulled the pin, and a whole bunch of other officers came. They threw me in the box.

A Stamp and a Bible

I was in the box for thirty days and thirty nights and in twenty-four-hour lockdown. I was full of self-pity, blaming everyone else, playing the victim. I was telling myself, "I don't deserve this. Why is this happening to me?" I was cursing out God, and I didn't care about anything anymore.

They locked me in and gave me my paper, an envelope, my pen, and my Bible. My sister had sent me my Bible early on in my incarceration, and I never picked it up. It was just a good-luck charm, I guess. It was something every inmate has in the corner of his cell. It was just there.

And then out of the blue, my sister wrote me and told me to read Psalm 91. I said, "Hell no, I'm not wasting my time with that." I didn't really want to touch the Bible, but I had nothing else to do. I opened up the Bible and started reading Psalm 91. A stamp fell out of my Bible. It was the stamp I needed to send out a ten-page letter I had written to my family. I wrote the letter to tell them that I messed up again and I was not coming home. I told them, "I'm probably going to do three more years in prison." I felt guilty, and I disappointed them another time. When that stamp fell out of my Bible, it was just like something weird happened to me. Goosebumps went throughout my body. Chills ran down my spine. This wasn't just any stamp. It was the stamp I needed to send my letter to my family.

I read the Bible from front to back while I was in there. I really began to understand what I was doing. For the first time, I understood the wrongdoing I was causing, not only for myself and my family but for the thousands of people I sold drugs to. I started to realize that they had families.

I did an extra ten months and came home on March 21, 2013. I came straight back to my neighborhood. I still have people walk up to me today and ask, "Do you still have this stash?"

And I say, "Get away from me with that." I don't even know where to find a cigarette.

ConBody

I came home, and I really believed. When I was in the cell, I drafted a spreadsheet of each exercise I was going to create for this boot camp and this fitness program I had in my head. And I said, "I'm going to make this happen." So when I came home, I just started helping people. I got a couple of people in the neighborhood and started working out with them for free in the park.

And then I bumped into Defy Ventures through another non-profit organization, and everything just kept falling into place. I feel like I'm just following the steps that God has put forth. I had no idea how to start a legit business, but they connected me with professionals who mentored me to get through the MBA-style program, which helped me develop the business plans and launch the business. I did well and won a competition pitching to investors.

I have gained a following of more than five thousand people and have hired seven people to teach my fitness classes. Five of them were formerly incarcerated. Today, this is my goal and movement that I'm creating through the blessings God has given me. I'm hiring as many formerly incarcerated individuals as I can to help place a dent in the recidivism rate and expand ConBody—not only nationally but internationally as well.

I have been featured in more than eighty articles, including eight pages in *Men's Fitness*, as well as TEDx, MSNBC, NPR, and the *New York Post*. God has greatly blessed me with the opportunities to share my story. All the glory goes to God for bestowing His amazing grace on me and empowering me in a miraculous way to positively impact the lives of thousands of others. Through God's unmerited grace, I have indeed been transformed.

Here is the second half of Psalm 91, the Scripture that helped save my life and led me to be a disciple of Christ:

> If you say, "The LORD is my refuge," and you make the Most High your dwelling, no harm will overtake you, no disaster will come near your tent. For he will command his angels concerning you to guard you in all your ways; they will lift you up in their hands, so that you will not strike your foot against a stone. You will tread on the lion and the cobra; you will trample the great lion and the serpent. "Because he loves me," says the LORD, "I will rescue him; I will protect him, for he acknowledges my name. He will call on me, and I will answer him; I will be with him in trouble, I will deliver him and honor him. With long life I will satisfy him and show him my salvation." (Psalm 91:9–16)

My Thoughts on Coss' Story

Like so many poverty-stricken youths today, Coss was determined never to be poor again. His determination essentially became an addiction to the accumulation of wealth and power. To him, the path to prosperity was through street crime. But despite his remarkable success in achieving wealth and power, his efforts hurt many others in his path and ultimately led to his own loss of freedom through incarceration—and an extreme personal crisis.

The real takeaway from this story is that the simple gift of the Holy Bible and the wisdom of someone who cared—his faithful sister—led him to read Psalm 91. We all should be mindful of the fact that we can access the Lord's healing and redemptive power and God's grace by committing to regularly reading His Word.

Time for Personal Reflection

1. Has something you've done ever caused other people harm, either directly or indirectly? If so, ask God to forgive you, and to give you the assurance that you can forgive yourself.

2. In prison, Coss realized how his drug activities had harmed his customers and their families. When he got out of prison, he devoted his time and energy to helping people get healthier. If you have harmed others at some point in your life, what can you do to reverse the damage and "make it right"?

3. God's grace enabled Coss to redirect his God-given gifts and talents away from evil and toward good. What do you think your God-given gifts and talents are? I'm convinced we all have them, and in using them for good, we can achieve true happiness. If you are puzzled by this question, consider taking a seminar or course on identifying your spiritual gifts. Then prayerfully consider how God would have you redirect your own actions and ambitions to make the best use of those gifts.

A Total Transformation:
From Addiction to Testimony

Kia Waller in 2016 at her twenty-year high school reunion.

Like many people who become addicted to drugs, Kia Waller of New Castle, Pennsylvania, says her addiction started with Percocet painkillers a pain-clinic doctor prescribed for her after she was in an automobile accident. Then she tried just about every other drug and became, in her words, "a garbage can." Long-term treatment in an in-patient recovery program finally ended her ten-year addiction.

She has regained the trust of her family and is now a Certified Recovery Specialist. She helps guide people into treatment and advises parents whose children are addicted to drugs.

My story about addiction is not typical. I grew up in a two-parent household. I was raised in church. I wasn't physically or sexually abused. I had a good upbringing, but addiction still found me.

What brought me to my knees was crack cocaine. It comes straight from hell. Toward the end, I was using opiates, benzos, alcohol, crack cocaine, and finally heroin because it's cheaper. I ended up being arrested on drug charges a couple of times because, like a lot of people, I was stealing to buy drugs. I would be on probation and try to get clean. I would go to twelve-step meetings and had every intention of quitting. But I would use again and fail my urine test, so I would get thrown in jail again.

As my addiction got worse, my actions became terrible. Between 2007 and 2013, I went to rehab eight times that I can remember. I kind of lost count after eight. And then I landed in prison. As of August 21,

2017, I have gone four years with no mood-altering substances. God poured His grace upon me because many times I should have been dead. I overdosed twice. Many times the devil was whispering in my ear, encouraging me to kill myself. Growing up, I knew that's something you don't do. I was putting myself in dangerous situations and disrespecting my body. I know for a fact that God was shielding me the whole time.

The Best Husband Anyone Could Have

My husband and I were high school sweethearts. We met when I was fourteen, and we got married when I was twenty-three. I am now thirty-nine years old. We have three daughters who are twenty-two, fifteen, and thirteen. We also have a six-year-old grandson and a granddaughter who was born at the end of August 2016.

For ten of our years together, I put that man through more than any person should have to endure. The last two years were absolutely terrible. I thank God for him because I never had to worry about my kids being in the foster care system or not being taken care of. When I was in prison and in the county jail, I met many women who either lost their children, didn't know where their children were, or were in the process of losing custody of them.

I didn't have to worry about that because my husband was always there to pick up the pieces. At the same time, he unknowingly enabled me for years because of his strong love for me. He didn't put money or drugs in my hand, but a lot of times our family members love us to death. They don't realize they are enabling us with their financial support and generosity.

He really tried, though. He tried being mean to me, and he tried being super nice. He tried just ignoring me. None of that worked. But toward the end, what did it was totally turning his back on me. He was loving me but fighting my addiction. So toward the end, I was totally alone. He actually picked up and moved out of the house we had lived in as a family for seven years. He took the kids and left. He did what he had to do to protect our children and to protect his heart because he was tired of getting it broken.

When I came home, things weren't perfect. Things still aren't perfect. But today, I honestly can say he trusts me again. He leaves his wallet out again. He trusts me to give me money for the bills again. There was a time when he had to sleep with his wallet in his pillowcase. And there was no way I was getting that bank information because he knew I would go clean out the account. He probably still carries some insecurities; it may never go away. But I know that the trust is building back up. I am so grateful for him.

Calling Out to God

I will never forget my last night of using. I choose to not forget it because I think that's one of the things that helps me stay on the right path. That last week, I was homeless. I was going days without showers. I had absolutely nobody. I had track marks all up and down my arms from the needle, and my left arm went totally numb for two days. I couldn't feel it. I didn't know if I had hit a nerve or what, but I was afraid to go to the hospital.

I was on the run from probation officers. It was ninety degrees in August, and I was walking around in a hooded jacket, afraid the police were going to see me. I was no longer welcome in my husband's new home, so I couldn't see my children. Toward the end, I was not welcome in my mother's home either. I was staying in trap houses, which are drug houses. There was no furniture in the one house I was staying in. It was infested with roaches and filthy.

On my last night of using, I broke into the vacant house that used to be our home. It was boarded up because the landlord was in Ecuador. I was sitting in what used to be my bedroom, alone. It was dark because there was no electricity. What was playing through my mind was something my husband had told me for years: "One day you're going to look up, and we're all going to be gone." I sat there on the floor, rocking back and forth, sobbing. I couldn't stop.

I got up on my knees and raised my hands. I was wailing, sobbing, and crying out loud for God to please help me. I prayed, "I don't care what, and I don't care how, but please help me, God. I can't do this anymore." Less than ten hours later, I was in jail.

When I walked in those doors to the county jail, I felt a sigh of relief. I could breathe because I knew that there was no way for me to get to any drugs, at least not right away. I didn't have to be scared anymore. I didn't have to put anything in me anymore. I made up my mind at that moment that that was it—I was done.

The Prison Recovery Program

After I spent a couple of months in the county jail, I ended up in Muncie State Prison for seven months. The prison has a program called Journey to Freedom that follows the Narcotics Anonymous format. It is a four-month-long, very intense drug and alcohol program, and it changed my life. I went into that program with the mind-set that I was going to take all from it that I could and try to better myself. I vowed to do everything that they told me to do. And I did. For those four months, I didn't even feel like I was in prison.

From eight in the morning until nine at night, we had round-the-clock rehabilitation. Besides a break for meals and a little free time, it's constant drug and alcohol care. The program is amazing. That is what gave me my push to not only stay on the right path, but to work on some things.

What I Learned about Myself

People continue to use because they're masking things that are bothering them inside, whether or not they are aware of it. During the program, I found out that deep down my insecurities kept me from fully loving myself. I was raised by a great stepfather who adopted me when I was six. Even though my life was very good, I didn't realize or accept the fact that my biological father, who is still alive and breathing and well today, chose not to be in my life.

Also, I had to deal with the insecurity I felt as a result of my husband cheating on me early in our relationship. I discovered that

I was masking that too. He would apologize, and I would go on like everything was perfect, when really, on the inside, I was still hurting. For years I felt that I was doing something wrong as a wife. But throughout that program, I learned that those were my husband's problems, his demons. I was doing everything I was supposed to do as a wife.

Those were some of the things that the Journey to Freedom program helped me bring out and work on. At the same time, I don't blame things that happened in the past for my addiction.

Helping Others in Early Recovery

God has turned my tests into testimony. Along with some other people in my church, I have started a Journey to Freedom recovery ministry. My pastor is not a recovering addict, but he's very passionate about it and is very supportive of those of us who are.

Also, I'm on the board of a group in New Castle that is getting ready to open a new recovery center in the community called Pathway to Freedom. Our goal is to reach out to all people affected by addiction, not just the addicts themselves. Sometimes people forget about that mother, that spouse, and that grandmother whose life is affected by addiction.

I'm also on a committee called Lights of Hope. I was one of the featured speakers at one of our recent candlelight vigils. People were there holding red candles for family members who are still in active addiction and black candles for people they've lost. I and many others were holding white candles to honor our own recovery. I told the group, "I realize now that I never surrendered my all. You cannot recover until you do so."

God's grace is so wonderful! I took a Certified Recovery Specialist (CRS) course and had been praying for an opportunity to get a full-time job that would enable me to help other women in recovery. On September 19, 2016, I became a full-time house manager of a women's sober living house in Youngstown, Ohio, called Gypsy House. It houses twelve women. I absolutely love my job! In

March 2017, I completed a Peer Support Specialist course in Canton, Ohio, and am now certified in Ohio and Pennsylvania. We are looking into opening another house in my hometown of New Castle, Pennsylvania.

I praise God that I am now making a career out of helping women who were struggling with addiction like I was. I feel like I have truly found my God-given purpose in life.

I also have a Facebook page and often communicate with people who are in active addiction, as well as parents whose children are going through it. New Castle is a small town, and a lot of people remember me during my worst times. I get a lot of messages that say, "I think my child's getting high, and I don't know what to do." I am able to lead them, guide them, and try to help them through it so they can get their children into treatment.

Here are just a few of the many Bible verses that helped Kia through that very difficult ten-year period:

> I can do all this through him who gives me strength. (Philippians 4:13)

> "No weapon forged against you will prevail, and you will refute every tongue that accuses you. This is the heritage of the servants of the LORD, and this is their vindication from me," declares the LORD. (Isaiah 54:17)

> As a prisoner for the Lord, then, I urge you to live a life worthy of the calling you have received. (Ephesians 4:1)

My Thoughts on Kia's Story

Kia's story carries messages for those suffering from addiction, as well as for their friends and family members.

As a parent or friend of someone who suffers from a serious addiction, you may relate to Kia's acknowledgment that friends and family members often enable a perpetuation of addictions through their well-intended love and generosity. After many attempts to reach out to help Kia, it wasn't until her husband took the drastic and difficult step of moving out with the kids to awaken Kia to her own reality.

Over time, Kia developed a remarkable self-awareness that ultimately enabled her to realize God's grace and fully recover from her crisis. She reached out, "wailing, sobbing, and crying out loud" in desperation to God with her prayers, but she also needed the ongoing support of the Journey to Freedom prison support group.

She declares, in her post-recovery ministry to others, that you must surrender your all, and you can't recover until you do. What wonderful advice for anyone reading her story who also is suffering from the crisis of addiction.

Time for Personal Reflection

1. Kia says, "People continue to use [drugs] because they're masking things that are bothering them inside, whether or not they are aware of it." Do you have memories of traumatic experiences hidden deep in your soul, causing continued pain and suffering in your life? Ask God to help you identify those hidden traumas and remove the mask (and hence, the burden) and believe that He will do so. Feel the liberating power of His outpouring of grace.

2. Are you carrying around insecurities and guilt that do not "belong" to you? Try to recognize if you are assuming the responsibility for problems that other people need to resolve. Then give it to God, surrender your all, and allow Him to heal you.

Out of the Ashes: Conquering Alcoholism

A 2015 article published in *The Washington Post* paints a grim picture of the prevalence of alcohol abuse in America:

> Alcohol is killing Americans at a rate not seen in at least thirty-five years, according to new federal data. [In 2014], more than 30,700 Americans died from alcohol-induced causes, including alcohol poisoning and cirrhosis, which is primarily caused by alcohol use. ... There were 9.6 deaths from these alcohol-induced causes per 100,000 people, an increase of 37 percent since 2002. ... More people died from alcohol-induced causes (30,722) than from overdoses of prescription painkillers and heroin combined (28,647), according to the CDC.[6]

This photo of Tina Stein, taken in February 2015, shows the joy associated with God's grace better than any words can describe–"out of the ashes," as she says.

Because alcohol addiction combines the elements of both mental illness and physical disease, alcoholism is classified as a substance abuse disorder in the *Diagnostic and Statistical Manual of Mental Disorders.*[7]

After a lonely childhood marred by her father's absence and her mother's mental illness, Tina Stein became an alcoholic as a teenager. Her downward spiral continued for three decades— and then she realized God's grace and "arose from the ashes."

I am fifty-two years old. I was born in Batavia, New York, and lived in a foster home from the age of one until the age of five while my mother was in a state hospital as the result of mental illness—depression. My father was completely absent because of alcoholism; I saw him only once a year. When I was five, my mother was released from the hospital, and she and my aunt went to pick me up from my foster home. I was told, "This is your mother." But I didn't know her, and I remember thinking, "Who are you, and where am I going?" Nobody gave me an insight into what was going on. I carried that with me for decades.

Needless to say, my home was not a healthy environment. I never felt like I belonged there. I was always searching outside of myself, way before I picked up a drink at the age of thirteen. So I was always at the neighbor's house or at a friend's house or down in the woods, playing with snails. I did not receive much affection or love, and I was an only child, so I was always a loner. I resented my mother for abandoning me.

I was raised Presbyterian; when I was young, my mother and aunt took me to church every Sunday. I have many fond memories of those times. I remember memorizing the books of the Bible and singing in the choir. I was baptized at the age of twelve on June 5, 1977. (I recently found my baptism certificate.)

My Search

I always searched outside my home for attention. As a result, I found alcohol and men at age thirteen. I always hung out with the older kids who drank and partied, like me. Once I discovered the effect that alcohol had on me, I drank to black out. I found that the stronger the alcohol, the faster I would get the effect. I also would use any substance (marijuana, hash, or speed) that would help get me to the point of feeling nothing. My goal was to be relieved of the pain.

I became an alcoholic and began to have blackouts regularly. At age sixteen, I quit high school and left home. I found a job in the restaurant business and continued that work, and my alcoholism, for thirty-three years. I had two failed marriages and two children—one from each marriage. After my second marriage ended, my alcohol use progressed. I found that it no longer altered my mood like it always had.

Both my marriages were affected by my alcoholism. I was very selfish and self-centered. I met both of my husbands in a bar, and they both drank like me. When I share my testimony, I say they were hostages, not husbands. It was all about me! I had to come to the realization that I could not love anyone till I loved myself, and that was accomplished only through God's love.

When my daughter was twenty and in college, my son was nine. One night, I called my son's dad and said, "You need to come get him. I can't do this to him anymore."

I found myself in an unhealthy relationship that led me to a crack cocaine addiction. I was smoking it daily and became homeless. I was dying inside. On December 6, 2007, I entered a drug-rehab facility. They gave me everything I needed to stay sober—God included—but I refused all of it. Then, while I was in an outpatient treatment program, I manipulated the system and was using cocaine. I got sober for seven months and then relapsed.

After two months of drinking, I awoke in the middle of the night with the thought that it would be a great idea to smoke some crack again. It felt like heaven and hell were fighting for me. I had tasted sobriety, but I chose to pick up a drink and a drug again. I kept using for two months and then overdosed on drugs.

My daughter was afraid for me, and her father once told me that she was going to leave school to find me. "Are you done yet?" he asked me. My reply was "No!"

Choosing Life

When I made it home, God came to me and asked me, "Do you want to live or die?" I chose life. I looked in the mirror and asked myself, "How did this happen again?" I truly felt that the Lord gave me the gift of surrender, and that night, I surrendered with my whole heart, being, mind, and soul, on my knees. I cried out, "God, help me!" His spirit came into me, and I immediately started to cry. It was like the floodgates opened. My heart, my soul, and my spirit just opened up. I hadn't cried in a long, long time. And the healing started at that moment. But I realized that God had been with me the whole time.

I called one of my ex-husbands and asked for help. I detoxed for three days and then entered an inpatient program on July 13, 2009.

Twenty-eight days later, on August 16, 2009, I accepted Jesus Christ as my Lord and Savior. Immediately I started reading the Bible and praying. After twenty-eight days in the clinic, I returned home

This photo of Tina was taken the day she entered rehab after a relapse on July 13, 2009.

and found my current church, where I made a public proclamation of my faith. Every morning I prayed to God, "Help me stay sober."

I have not picked up any substance by the grace of God since! The difference this time was that I truly surrendered on my knees with a true heart and asked God to help me.

From Shame to Service and Success

The worst parts of my alcoholism were the guilt, shame, and remorse. For thirty-three years, I was always thinking about drinking—what I was going to drink, who I was going to drink with, and how I was going to get the next drink. I experienced a total loss of control. My mornings were full of despair, and I had no memory of what happened the night before. And when alcohol stopped having an effect on me, I turned to crack. That drug led to even more darkness and despair and another level of remorse, shame, and guilt. I sold my soul to get the next fix. I would go to any length to get my next one. At the end of my addiction, my body would go into withdrawal if I didn't get alcohol or drugs. It is glorious to be free from that burden.

About a year into my sobriety, I heard God say to me, "I've given to you so freely; it is time for you to give back." For six years, I have volunteered with the Good News Jail and Prison Ministry. God opened the door for me to start an alumni meeting in the rehab facility where I found God.

Today I have a beautiful life. I love myself. Both of my children are proud of me, and I am present in their lives. My daughter says she gets her strength from me. That is a true gift from God.

Two years ago, I bought a home as a single mother. When I got sober, I found myself $30,000 in debt, but I am debt-free today. I have an amazing job in the road-construction business as a safety supervisor. In 2011, I completed my GED. All these blessings are from having a daily relationship with Jesus Christ and giving back to others the same type of support He led me to. I love Jesus Christ with all my heart and soul. He did save a wretch like me!

Healing My Resentment

I believe the seed was planted for my realization of God's grace when I went to church as a young girl. I have since gone back to that church for services and felt many fond memories come rushing back. I even felt the presence of the Spirit to help me remember when I was baptized.

When I was nineteen, I went to see my mother, whose health was failing. I asked her why she put me in a foster home. She explained it to me, but I did not fully understand it. So years after my mother died and I had gained sobriety, I went back to see the daughter of my foster parents, who had already passed away. I asked her what happened when I was a year old. The daughter told me, "You see that house across the street? You and your mom lived there when she got sick. She knew my mom was a foster parent, so she came and asked if we could take you in."

At that moment, I was healed and delivered from my resentment. I felt peace and comfort that my mom didn't abandon me; she found me a safe place to live. At that moment, God allowed me to forgive my mother and my aunt. I realized that they did the best they could with what they had. They obviously were suffering themselves.

Tina says the following Bible verses are the ones she has always turned to during the times when she felt like she needed to be reminded that God's grace is there for her and always has been:

> I can do all this through him who gives me strength. (Philippians 4:13)

> Be strong and courageous. Do not be afraid or terrified because of them, for the LORD your God goes with you; he will never leave you nor forsake you. (Deuteronomy 31:6)

> In all these things we are more than conquerors through him who loved us. (Romans 8:37)

My Thoughts on Tina's Story

Tina spent time in a foster home when she was very young, and she never felt like she fit in anywhere. Drinking as a young teenager helped her feel like one of the crowd. Like many people with addictions, Tina was trapped in a vicious cycle—the more she drank and did drugs, the worse she felt about herself. As she says, "The worst parts of my alcoholism were the guilt, shame, and remorse." Those emotions drove her deeper into her addiction.

Without the grace of God and a full surrender to His will, it is nearly impossible to overcome a thirty-year addiction. As Tina said, relapses are common. Even though a person might want desperately to stop drinking or using, she is powerless to do so by herself. But Tina is living proof that God can defeat even the most gripping addiction—if the person in crisis surrenders fully to Him. She said, "The difference this time was that I truly surrendered on my knees with a true heart and asked God to help me."

God wants us to give Him the addiction or other crisis in our lives and trust that He has the power and desire to conquer its influence over us. He wants us to submit our lives to Him fully.

Time for Personal Reflection

1. Have you ever felt abandoned by anyone? If so, did you later ask that person or someone else about the situation, like Tina did? Understanding the driving forces behind our addictions by taking the direct approach and getting more information about what happened can be illuminating and healing. Sometimes our memories of an event are not accurate. Talking it out with a friend or a medical professional and resolving the mystery behind the situation can be the first step to forgiveness and healing.

2. As a child, Tina said she felt like she didn't belong in her home, so she searched outside her home and herself to find acceptance. Did you or anyone you know ever have a similar experience? What do you think parents, teachers, and other adults can do to recognize such despair in children and then take preventative measures to steer them in the right direction?

3. Tina's story shows her progression from addiction to relapses to sobriety and then to the healing of relationships, forgiveness, and service to others. Tina heard God ask her if she wanted to live or die. Her recovery started when, on her knees, she surrendered her entire being, heart, soul, and mind to Him. So often, before we resort to potentially terminal self-destructive behaviors, God's grace arrives to save us when we simply surrender to Him and acknowledge that we can't go on without Him.

Divine Intervention:
Drug Abuse and God's Voice

Jess Libby is pictured with her husband, Rob, who was her childhood sweetheart. He is the director of the Celebrate Recovery program at their church, and Jess is a sponsor in that program. She has been heroin-free for four years.

Jessica Libby's decades-long drug abuse was precipitated when she was a toddler and experienced a lot of family drama. She developed an eating disorder and began looking for trouble while still in middle school. Then came the full-blown drug abuse, which spiraled out of control as Jess experienced sixteen miscarriages, a suicide attempt, and some abusive relationships.

With the Lord's help, Jess turned her life around and is now a happy, healthy wife and mom who is active in her church and works with recovering drug addicts. Her story is a testament to the fact that Jesus is a force mighty enough to turn around a life that seems destined for destruction.

Here is Jess' story.

I was born in 1980 to an abusive, alcoholic dad and a workaholic mom. At the age of three, I was awoken one night by loud banging and my mom pleading for it to stop. A faint voice instructed me to get up and go into the kitchen. When I walked in, I saw that my dad had my mom up against the wall, clutching her by the throat. Scared and confused, I asked my mom if she was OK. She choked out "Yes" and told me to go back to bed; my dad didn't even acknowledge me. While heading back to bed, I heard my mom hit the floor and gasp for air. As I lay in bed, my mind was flooded with thoughts of guilt, shame, regret, and fear. That night my road of self-destruction began.

I began using food as a way to relieve stress, eating butter dipped in sugar, pickle sandwiches, and mixing Kool-Aid with milk. I knew it wasn't right, but it made me feel better. My whole world was based on my appearance and earning my dad's love and acceptance. He was very critical of my appearance, and I began the battle of anorexia at the age of eight. He thought it was cute that I was concerned with my appearance at such a young age.

A Safe, Fun Place

The older I got, the more I got the itch to do things I knew I shouldn't. By the age of nine, I was smoking daily, drinking alcohol on occasion, starving myself to be thin, and smoking marijuana. I enjoyed school. I could pretend to be someone I wasn't when I was at school—to the point where I would put a change of clothes in my bag every morning to change upon arrival. But I wasn't one to get in trouble at school. My teachers adored me, and I had plenty of friends, including a boy named Rob, whom I met at age seven. He always made me feel special. It was like I had two lives, and I tried very hard to keep them separate. I didn't like taking friends to my house for fear that they would see that my dad was drunk. My best friend, Amanda, whom I met at age eight, was an exception to my rule. She was a friend I could relate to.

Over the next two years, during a lot of family drama, I fell further down a destructive path. I started using alcohol and speed on a regular basis. I learned how to sneak out my second-story bedroom window and how to sneak boys in. I began getting in trouble at school and was kicked off the cheering squad when a friend and I showed up for practice half an hour late with alcohol on our breath. I switched schools when I was thirteen and was reunited with Rob, who had my heart, and Amanda, who was my partner in crime.

A Suicide Attempt, a Baby Boy, and Abusive Relationships

My mother decided she and I would move to Florida to be with my dad. I was so angry with her that I attempted suicide by taking a whole bottle of Tylenol. I was violently ill for twenty-four hours. My mom was absolutely disgusted with me, and we never spoke of the incident again.

For the next three years in Florida, I had no interest in school. I got high with friends and spent the afternoons going to bars for happy hour with my dad. Then I met a guy. He was a senior who had that tough-guy look, wore cowboy boots, and drove a truck. He knew just what to say and do. I was hooked. I stopped smoking marijuana, drinking, and hanging out with my friends because he didn't like it. He wanted me with him every second of every day. He said he loved me and wanted to have a family. At fifteen years old, on Mother's Day, I had to tell my mom I was pregnant. My dad begged me to have an abortion. He explained that he knew how difficult it was, having been a parent at sixteen himself, but I was already at twelve weeks, so an abortion wasn't an option. On December 15, 1996, my beautiful, healthy son made his way into the world. At one ounce shy of six pounds, he was perfect. I swore I would give David Jr. everything I never had.

A few months later, David Jr. and I moved in with his dad, David Sr. He became very controlling and emotionally, physically, and sexually abusive. I did everything to hide it. I felt I deserved it, and I didn't want my son to be without his dad. One night after putting David Jr. to bed, I went to bed too. David Sr. kicked me from head to toe with steel-toed boots—just because he didn't want me to go to sleep. David Jr. woke up and came to try and help me. Looking at his little face took me back to when I was three and my dad had my mom by the throat. I knew I had to get out.

My dad bought David Jr. and me plane tickets to Maine, and my mom handled the legal piece. I never went back. My biggest fear became a reality: my son didn't have a father, and I was alone. But at least I had my son.

In Maine, I was able to connect with my childhood bestie, but my childhood sweetie, Rob, had already enlisted in the Marines. Though I was disappointed that I couldn't be with him, I was happy for him and his success. He had already been promoted twice. I learned to accept the fact that I would probably never see him again and that he was better off without me.

I soon found a new addiction, Xenadrine. It's an ephedrine-based diet pill that's available at many stores. My appearance obsession hit a whole new level. I was working out two to three times a day, and both anorexia and bulimia got a tight grip on me. Within two months, I could wear my two-year-old son's belts—but still thought I was fat.

I met another man, and it was a roller coaster ride for three years. Shortly after we got married, he became abusive to my son, yet I still let him convince me to go back to him. After a night of drinking, he raised a glass to hit me. He was a small man, so I laid him out and left him face-down in the hallway to sleep it off. The next morning, I left and never went back. We were divorced four months later.

The Loss of an Infant Daughter, Sixteen Miscarriages, and a Cancer Diagnosis

Just one week after leaving husband number one, I hooked up with yet another guy. He was my age, came from a good family, had never been married, had no kids, and David Jr. liked him. He introduced me to a whole new party scene … cocaine. I had been completely against it, but now it just seemed fun. We dated for two short months before David and I moved in with him.

Two short months after that, I learned I was pregnant. Though the news was unexpected, we took it well and became excited. But at three months, I miscarried. I was devastated. After two more miscarriages, I delivered my baby girl, Gracey, on March 4, 2004, four weeks premature. She weighed just four pounds and twelve ounces. She had a cleft lip and a cleft palate, and her windpipe was a third of the size it should have been. After my tiny baby endured two open-heart surgeries, a nurse came in to tell us our daughter had passed. I had to say good-bye. As I held her one last time, blood trickled from her mouth, an image I desperately wanted to escape. The sweet smell of her soapy-clean skin lingered in my nose. The pain was too great. I allowed myself to die with her that day.

Gracey's dad became husband number two. We never really discussed what happened or how we felt about it. We both hit the self-destruct express lane. Cocaine became an every-weekend occurrence. I became obsessed with becoming pregnant, but every miscarriage set me further back. After my sixteenth miscarriage, the doctors told me another pregnancy could kill me, and it was time to be done. My second husband didn't take the news well. I had had enough and left him. Out of guilt, I continued to have relations with husband number two through the holidays. He had already started dating someone else, but I learned I was pregnant. Knowing I would miscarry anyway, I continued with all my recreational habits. On September 16, our beautiful miracle baby, Dani Jean, made her way into the world. There were some complications, but she was born perfectly healthy. She didn't experience drug withdrawals or have any effects from my drug use—another secret I would bury.

After a minor car accident, I began taking pain pills and muscle relaxers. For three years, the number of meds, the strengths, and the doses all increased. In addition to my prescriptions, I was buying pills from newly made friends. Then my doctor finally realized I had a problem. In just over three months' time, I had spent almost $11,000 on oxycodone. I was starting to see that I had a problem, and so was everyone else. Drugs even came between me and my bestie since the age of eight, Amanda, and we went our separate ways.

Not long after that, I was diagnosed with cervical cancer and was scheduled for a full hysterectomy. I was a thirty-year-old single mom of two, unemployed, and now I had cancer. On Christmas Day, we moved in with my parents once again. One of my suppliers was now offering heroin. I had said I would never do it, but it was cheaper, stronger, and lasted twice as long as cocaine. At first, a bag would last me four days, but it wasn't long before four days turned to one.

Reunion and New Life

One day I received an unexpected message from Rob, my childhood sweetheart. After ten years of searching, I had found him on

Facebook. We began talking daily and catching up with each other. He too had been twice divorced and had three children. He was now retired from the USMC and considering moving to Maine. In October 2013, Rob came back home to visit his mom for a couple of weeks. Soon I had plans to meet with Rob. My dealer had been out of heroin for a day, and I wasn't able to get my fix. On the verge of withdrawals and exhausted, I contemplated canceling. Then I heard that faint voice telling me this could be my last chance to ever see Rob. I tried to make myself look halfway decent, grabbed a six-pack, and went to see him at his dad's house.

The first thing he said was, "Wow, you look tired." He had no idea! As he talked about some of the places he had been and things he had done, I was thinking I needed to run the other way. He was a good guy, and I would crush him. But neither of us wanted the night to end. We went back to my place and stayed up all night talking and laughing. I forgot all about not having a fix. We spent the remainder of his visit together. I opened up to him about my drug use and told him it was my life and I could never give it up. I told him that I wasn't the same girl he used to know and that life had changed me. I told him it would be in his best interest to go the other way, but he insisted that the little girl he had known was still in there, and he let me know he wasn't going anywhere. He knew just what to say and just what to do. It was like he was reading my mind, to the point it actually creeped me out a few times.

When his stay came to an end, it was hard to say good-bye again, but Rob planned to return in February for good. Within a week, he had his truck packed, and he was back on my doorstep. I now had everything I ever wanted in a man.

While serving in Iraq, Rob had been involved in an explosion and sustained severe injuries. Part of his pain management for a broken back was morphine. He stopped taking his meds. I watched him suffer through the withdrawals and tried to help him. I started thinking twice every time I got high. I started feeling guilty for getting high. Even though he had a legit reason to take the meds, he gave them up and endured the pain. I didn't have physical pain anymore, so why did I need the drugs? When Rob asked me, "Why do you get high?" I didn't really know. I attempted to stop on my own a few times but never made it through the first twenty-four hours.

One day, I sat in the Veterans Administration parking lot waiting for Rob to finish his doctor's appointment. I tried to figure out why I needed heroin but couldn't get past the feeling of needing a fix. When Rob returned to the truck, I explained to him that I wasn't ready to go without it and that I needed it. Every excuse I came up with, he had a solution. The next day, completely frustrated, sick, and angry, I went and got wasted the first chance I got. I left my five-year-old daughter sitting in my truck and was late to drop her off to her dad on his birthday. As I said good-bye to her, I saw the look of fear on her dad's face, and things started to become clear. What if I had been busted by the cops? What if my daughter knew what I was doing? I finally realized the danger I was putting my kids in. As I got in my truck, the tears began to fall. I was overwhelmed with guilt and shame. What had I done?

What No Drug Can Ever Match

I tried to drink the feelings away, but it didn't help. Rob met me at home and tried talking to me. I called my uncle, who was a pastor, and he arrived at our apartment within thirty minutes. He spoke to both Rob and me. He informed Rob that he needed to remove all drugs and alcohol from the apartment. He left books for me to read and prayed with us. On January 27, 2014, I put drugs up my nose for the last time. I was severely ill for two weeks; Rob stayed with me 24/7. When I was finally well enough to leave the house, my first stop was a Celebrate Recovery meeting. In small group, I heard women sharing all the wonderful things Jesus Christ had been doing in their lives. I, too, wanted to feel that power. That night in closing prayer, I asked Jesus Christ into my heart. It was a feeling no drug could ever replicate. My light had been relit! For three days, I confessed hateful sins from my tongue. I begged for forgiveness.

Not only was I forgiven; I was shown mercy, love, and grace. God revealed that the faint voice I had heard all those years was His all along. He reminds me often that He saved my life for a reason. I felt as though a bright light filled me. I went home feeling good for the first time in a long time. God provided me strength to not use drugs, and with every day I remained sober, His strength became stronger.

The next morning, I woke before sunrise, full of energy and excited to start the day. This was not my character at all. I had half the apartment clean before the sun came up. When Rob got up, he was amazed. He looked at me and said, "I knew it would happen. I just didn't know it would happen this fast!" For three days, Rob heard of all the horrible things I had done and all the horrible things that had been done to me. I slept well for the first time in a long time, relieved of the burden of my secrets. We set a wedding date, exchanged vows, and became one with God.

Rob and I are now married, and God has led me to make many amends. I have received forgiveness from both my children and have regained their trust. I now have a friendly relationship with my ex-husband and his wife. I have a very close relationship with both my mother and my middle sister, and they too have grown closer to God by watching all that He continues to do in me. And, after many months of praying, God brought Amanda back into my life, and we now travel the road of recovery together.

Now, as a care minister and Celebrate Recovery sponsor in my church, I work directly with recovering addicts and help them find their way from darkness to the light of Jesus. I meet with them one-on-one at least once a week, teach lessons at our open group, and help lead a small study group. In early 2018, by the grace of God, I will celebrate four years of being clean and sober. It is only by God and through Christ. I am truly forgiven.

Jess says this passage from the book of Psalms is among the Scriptures that remind her to put her hope in Him when she does not feel strong:

"Israel, put your hope in the LORD, for with the LORD is unfailing love and with him is full redemption. He himself will redeem Israel from all their sins" (Psalm 130:7–8).

She adds that during her darkest hours, the Serenity Prayer was her lifesaver. She said it a minimum of ten times a day in the beginning of her journey:

> God grant me the serenity
> to accept the things I cannot change;
> courage to change the things I can;
> and wisdom to know the difference.
> Living one day at a time;
> Enjoying one moment at a time;
> Accepting hardships as the pathway to peace;
> Taking, as He did, this sinful world
> as it is, not as I would have it;
> Trusting that He will make all things right
> if I surrender to His Will;
> That I may be reasonably happy in this life
> and supremely happy with Him
> Forever in the next.
> Amen.
> —Reinhold Niebuhr

My Thoughts on Jess' Story

Jess' story is one of many examples of the way God places people in our lives to guide us. Sometimes those people come and go throughout our lives, like her husband, Rob, did—they became childhood friends at age seven and are now married. Or like the uncle who prayed with and for her during her darkest hour.

Jess endured unspeakable loss, sorrow, and pain her entire life—from seeing her father assault her mother at age three, to suffering sixteen miscarriages, to holding her infant daughter as she died, to surviving her own bout with cancer. Jess is like so many of us who sense the Lord's presence during our darkest hours but do not always realize it is Him until much later. She said, "God revealed that the faint voice I had heard all those years was His all along."

After trying to quit her drug addiction for decades, God finally gave her the strength and will to quit. He can deliver us from the ravages of addiction and other crises.

Time for Personal Reflection

1. Jess' childhood sweetheart and now husband, Rob, came back into her life at the exact moment when she needed him. Has God ever placed someone or something phenomenal in your path right when you were about to give up? If so, did you realize it was part of God's plan, or did you think it was a coincidence? Now, after reading Jess' story, what do you think?

2. Jess' contentment and happiness after enduring all the painful life challenges she experienced is a testament to the power of God's loving grace. Do you know someone who has gone through what seems like more than his or her share of crises in life, or have you? To what extent does Jess' story give you hope?

Healing Insights

- Your personally painful experiences are often hidden deep within your psyche. Left unaddressed, they can lead to stronger and more dangerous addictions. Jesus will help you to identify and uncover those painful experiences.

- Jesus brings a force powerful enough to help you overcome the temptation to engage in behaviors that are not aligned with His plan for your life. Depending on the situation, as a recovering addict, you also may require medical treatment, behavioral therapy, and/or counseling to uncover the root causes of the addiction. Often this requires intervention by friends or family.

- Be bold and specific in your prayer requests to the Lord. Stand on His biblical promises and expect miraculous answers to your prayers.

- Recognize that you aren't strong enough to overcome the powerful grip of addiction. Tell the Lord you desperately need Him to be in control of your life, and He will be there. Surrender your all to Him.

- In recovery, you need to identify your God-given talents and redirect them away from evil purposes and into good purposes.

- Intertwined with addiction are damaging emotions like guilt, shame, anger, and an inability to forgive (either yourself or others). It is important to acknowledge and address these manifestations of your addiction. Addiction ruins not only the lives of those who are addicted to a substance or activity; it also can ruin the lives of the people around them. Healing requires making amends to those who have been affected negatively by your addiction.

A Prayer for Those Struggling with Addictive Behaviors

If you are suffering from some form of addiction that is ruining your life and you are finding it impossible to resist the temptation, make a daily habit of fervent prayers for relief. Here is a prayer you can modify to reflect your specific situation and then repeat often. Make further modifications that incorporate thankfulness as God's loving grace begins to heal you.

Loving and gracious God. I am reaching out to You now because I cannot overcome my addiction to _____. I want to be free of my compulsive behaviors that I can't seem to control, no matter how hard I try.

I pray that You will give me the strength to overcome and resist the temptations to repeat my self-destructive behaviors. I trust You and stand on Your promises to never forsake or leave me. I need You to begin to heal me now and lead me away from my addiction through Your love and grace.

In Jesus' name I pray. Amen.

4

HEALING FROM EMOTIONAL AND PHYSICAL ISSUES

People who suffer from either physical or emotional pain often feel isolated because they feel others don't understand what they are experiencing. Those who do not feel pain sometimes become impatient with those who do, and that can cause the person with pain to suffer in silence.

Physical and/or emotional pain is a symptom of just about any health issue, whether it's heart disease, cancer, PTSD, or depression. First, consider the incidence rates of physical pain among adults in the United States. According to the 2011 Gallup-Healthways Well-Being Index:

> More than one in five adults in their late 40s through late 80s has some type of recurring physical pain. ... Chronic pain conditions increase rapidly from about ages 25 to 60, after which reports of chronic pain increase only slightly. Americans' reports of chronic pain conditions increase most sharply from their mid-20s to late 50s. This is likely related to the repeated use of muscles, joints, and ligaments over time,

as well as this age group's increased likelihood of being over-weight or obese.[1]

Emotional pain can be just as debilitating. A 2014 *Psychology Today* article listed five ways in which emotional pain can be worse than physical pain. For example, memories can trigger emotional pain but not physical pain. And emotional pain can damage our self-esteem and long-term mental health.[2]

But most people are more inclined to seek medical attention for a physical injury than for an emotional issue. Because emotional issues are less apparent to friends and family, many people think they are less urgent. It is important to recognize the potentially debilitating effects of emotional pain. Left untreated, it can lead to self-harm such as cutting, overeating, and drug and alcohol abuse. It also can lead to suicide.

One way to reduce the likelihood of health problems of any kind in retirement is to delay retirement for at least a year. A study published in the *Journal of Epidemiology and Community Health* in 2016 found that healthy adults who delayed retirement for one year past age sixty-five had an 11 percent lower risk of dying. Why? In an interview with *US News & World Report*, the lead author of the study, Chenkai Wu, explained it this way: "Delayed retirement ... could potentially mean keeping cognitively and physically active and socially engaged, [which] may, at least partially, help delay the onset of that decline."[3]

The Bible is a welcome source of comfort for people experiencing both physical and emotional pain. Here are just a few encouraging verses to turn to when seeking relief from pain:

Therefore we do not lose heart. Though outwardly we are wasting away, yet inwardly we are being renewed day by day. (2 Corinthians 4:16)

For just as we share abundantly in the sufferings of Christ, so also our comfort abounds through Christ. If we are distressed, it is for your comfort and salvation; if we are comforted, it is for your comfort, which produces in you patient endurance of the same sufferings we suffer. (2 Corinthians 1:5–6)

But rejoice inasmuch as you participate in the sufferings of Christ, so that you may be overjoyed when his glory is revealed. (1 Peter 4:13)

I consider that our present sufferings are not worth comparing with the glory that will be revealed in us. (Romans 8:18)

Resist him, standing firm in the faith, because you know that the family of believers throughout the world is undergoing the same kind of sufferings. And the God of all grace, who called you to his eternal glory in Christ, after you have suffered a little while, will himself restore you and make you strong, firm and steadfast. (1 Peter 5:9–10)

He will wipe every tear from their eyes. There will be no more death or mourning or crying or pain, for the old order of things has passed away. (Revelation 21:4)

Victory in Christ: A Vietnam Veteran Serves Others

Bob Uber

The trauma that military personnel witness during combat is so horrific that it can haunt their memories, rob them of sleep, and wound them for life, both physically and emotionally. Those who have never been in combat cannot fathom how debilitating it can be to face imminent death for prolonged periods of time, survive when beloved comrades do not, witness the carnage of children, and then return to former lifestyles feeling like no one understands.

According to the National Institute of

Health's National Institute of Mental Health webpage, "people with PTSD [post-traumatic stress disorder] may startle easily, become emotionally numb (especially in relation to people to whom they used to be close), lose interest in things they used to enjoy ... be irritable [and] become more aggressive ... They avoid situations that remind them of the original incident and often find anniversaries of the incident to be very difficult." They may also have trouble falling asleep and staying asleep.[4]

A veteran does not have to be injured to have PTSD; being exposed to horrible and life-threatening experiences and/or seeing other people injured or killed can lead to PTSD. PTSD is a wound to the mind. It is the result of a crisis, and the mind struggles to process a crisis. It is like sticking a square peg in a round hole. The most common self-treatment for PTSD is consuming drugs and alcohol because they anesthetize the mind.

The US Department of Veterans Affairs estimates that PTSD has afflicted 30 percent of Vietnam veterans, as many as 12 percent of Gulf War (Desert Storm) veterans, 11 percent of veterans of the war in Afghanistan, and 11 to 20 percent of Iraqi war veterans.[5]

Bob Uber was diagnosed with PTSD decades after he returned home from Vietnam. His thirteen-month tour of duty in Vietnam began when he was twenty-four years old. He was subjected to enemy fire from the North Vietnamese the first day he arrived at his post. He witnessed devastation that no one should ever have to see, and those images will haunt his memory forever.

In 2011, Bob established Heal Our Heroes (healourheroes.org), an organization in High Point, North Carolina, that provides support, camaraderie, and outdoor retreats that aim to help veterans heal. Bob finds strength in helping other veterans ease their suffering. As debilitating as his wartime experience was, he sees that God is using it—and him—to support veterans in a way that only a veteran of a foreign war can do.

Here is Bob's story.

The Most Horrifying Carnage

During my thirteen-month tour of duty in Vietnam, I was a commissioned officer. My specialty was Military Intelligence (MI), so I was assigned to be a senior interrogation officer in Saigon.

However, at that precise time, the US Department of Defense and those who were running the war decided we needed to demonstrate to the American people that we were winning the war. That meant we would turn the military operations over to the Vietnamese. As part of that effort, they moved large units out of the southern region of Vietnam and began putting together combat advisory teams—teams of three men who were "embedded" as advisors in villages and communities all over the area known as the Delta. As I was on my flight from California to Saigon, my orders were changed.

I spent a whole year "embedded" with two other Americans. We lived among the Vietnamese, ate their food, and trained them in both military operations and civil affairs. On the day I arrived at my duty

Bob in a Vietnamese village shortly after his arrival.

assignment deep in the village, I sat down to write a letter to my wife. I wrote, "Here I am. The journey has begun. Pray for me. I don't know what to expect." Someone turned on a projector with a large seven-inch reel to watch a movie. At that moment, I heard a distinct whistling sound I became all too familiar with. I quickly learned that it meant incoming mortar rounds. We were under attack within four hours of my arrival at my post.

We ran to our bunkers for security. The enemy's tactic was to shoot four or five random mortars before we discovered their location and then run. It just happened that one of those rounds hit our ammo dump, where we stored all our munitions. So one round became one thousand. For the next six hours, it "cooked off," which is the term for bullets, hand grenades, and mortar storage firing off. When we were finally able to leave our bunker, I was forever imprinted with the most horrific, devastating carnage I think is known to man. There would be a temporary lull, so people would go out into the compound, thinking it was safe, and another round of mortars would hit them.

The gruesome images I saw that day were seared into my mind, and they will remain for the rest of my life. When a bomb or hand grenade went off in the midst of a group, there was carnage—absolute devastation. We spent the next several days putting people in body bags, trying to make identifications, and trying to see if there were any survivors. What was most devastating, and became the core of my trauma, were the children. Children are not supposed to die; the adults who sign up to fight our wars are, but not children. All my nightmares and all my flashbacks involve seeing children as carnage, as collateral damage to war. That will never go away. That is one of my many, many issues.

Facing Survivor's Guilt

When I was a captain, I worked with a major to identify the Viet Cong (VC) leaders. They looked like everyday people, but we knew they were leaders of the military's infrastructure. I had identified a very significant individual, one of the top three leaders in the Viet Cong. He was my target.

As I was about to head out on my mission, a message came down from headquarters saying we needed a show of force to the enemy. They wanted a big operation. The major came to me and asked, "Do you have any missions or targets?"

I said, "Absolutely. I have a very high-value target."

He said, "Well, we're going to take on a bigger mission. We're not going to arrest him. We're going to go out with a show of force, lots of soldiers, lots of military, and start rounding people up."

My response neared insubordination. I said, "Sir, that's my mission. I know him. I've seen him. I have identified him. I've begun to identify his patterns."

The major replied, "I know. Just give me the intel, and we'll take over."

When one of us was out, another one of us would stay up all night with the radio, ready for search and rescue and quick response, in case there was an incident. The major proceeded outside our compound gate less than one hundred yards in his vehicle and hit an IED (Improvised Explosive Device). He, along with my interpreter and radio man, whom he had taken with him, were blown into oblivion. It was a direct assault. They drove right over the IED, and it detonated.

So another nightmare for me, and another challenge mentally, is "survivor's guilt." I was supposed to be on that mission, and I was supposed to be the one in that Jeep. I had fought for that. I had challenged the major's right to usurp my mission. I asked God, "Why not me, and why him?"

Appropriating Grace

While I was in Vietnam, on several occasions, my wife would hear a dog barking in the middle of the night. She would get up to try to quiet the dog and see what the disturbance was, but there was no barking dog. She began to understand that it was God's call to prayer, for her to appropriate God's grace for my safety.

Also, the phone would ring at odd hours, and she'd pick up the phone and say, "Hello? Hello?" Nobody was there. Again, she would fall to her knees and pray for God to place a hedge of protection around me.

When I came back, we started comparing notes because it was so bizarre to her. It turns out that, without exception, all the times those things happened were times that I was in harm's way. God's grace can be appropriated through the prayers of others, and I think it saved my life.

Touching Vietnamese Children's Lives

My mother was just marvelous. She was my hero in a thousand different ways. She wanted to be a missionary, so she lived out the life of a missionary vicariously through me. I'm the youngest of seven, her baby boy. It helped that I'm fairly verbal, so I could tell her stories like this, and she would just weep openly with absolute joy.

One of the greatest expressions of God's grace in my lifetime was her great passion for children. She taught children's Sunday school for fifty years. She said, "Bob, I know why you're over there. You are a missionary paid by the government. You should stay a second year."

I said, "Well, I'm not sure I see it that way. I don't think my wife would like that idea."

But Mom did. She began to send me little things that children would enjoy, such as scribble pads. If you scribbled over the paper with a pencil, an image would appear. They were images based on the Bible, such as Noah's ark or King David. The children in Vietnam were captivated by them. God also impressed upon my mother to send coloring books to Vietnam. So she did. They were filled with pictures like Jesus the Good Shepherd, Jesus carrying a lamb to safety, and children sitting on Jesus' lap.

The children cherished those coloring books beyond words. And to my shame, because it bordered on child labor, for one page torn out of the coloring book, they would wash and clean my Jeep and do all my chores. When my fellow soldiers and I would go to the little canteens where you could have a snack, we'd look inside, and one of those colored pictures would be hanging on the wall.

The other plan my mother had was to order five thousand copies of the gospel of John in Vietnamese. She ordered them the first month I was there. But because of a printer strike or a dock strike or

These Vietnamese children are enjoying the Bible-based coloring books that Bob's mother sent to Vietnam from America.

spiritual warfare, they did not arrive in Vietnam until three weeks before I was to return to the States. One day, unannounced, an American truck pulled up. It was the mail truck. And out came forty boxes of the gospel of John—five thousand copies.

Trying to figure out how to distribute these booklets seemed like an impossible task. I thought, "I'll go up in a helicopter and drop them from the sky." I was in a helicopter every five days on air mobile combat missions to secure areas and build outposts as part of our defensive structure. We always went out into "high op tempo," a term for the medivac used to transport the wounded. I kept forgetting to take those boxes with me so that I could dump them out the sides of the helicopter like propaganda.

Disciples to Deliver God's Message

One evening, a defining event happened. The Vietnamese commander did a draft, or conscription. That means he rounded up every able-bodied male who was not in uniform and signed them up to serve for one year. After the military processed these South Vietnamese men at headquarters, they were left to mingle and wander around our compound until the following morning, when they would be shipped out for training and then inserted into the war.

They looked like a flock of wandering sheep, candidly. After dinner, I was sitting there watching them, and God said, "Hello, you have forty boxes of the Good News." I opened one box and took out a handful of the gospel of John booklets. But my interpreter wasn't there, and I didn't speak the language. So I was a little bit paralyzed. I wouldn't call it chicken, but I would call it hesitant. My dear little friend, a Vietnamese girl who was about ten years old, was there. Her name was Biet Nungh, and she was a treasure of a little gal. She always found me, and when she would show up, twenty other kids would come with her. She became the leader of the pack, and I became the pied piper.

As I was pulling booklets out of the box, Biet Nungh came up to me and asked in Vietnamese, "What are you doing? Can we play? Do you have anything to color?" She communicated with me using unofficial sign-language communication. I thought, "Aha, here's my answer." I gave her five or six copies of the gospel of John. Using hand signals, I told her, "You go give them out" because I was still appropriately hesitant to do it myself. Without hesitation, she walked over and started handing out the gospel of John to the wandering sheep who were in the compound. And quickly, my greatest fear—a near night-mare—occurred when she started pointing at me, saying to them, "He's got the mother lode. Go see him." When I would not go to them, by God's grace, they came to me. They each received a copy of the gospel of John in Vietnamese. To God's glory, they sat for three hours transfixed and prayerfully transformed by reading through those lit-tle gospels of John until it was too dark to read.

Biet Nungh (left), Bob's ten-year-old Vietnamese "disciple," is shown with another Vietnamese child.

A group of Vietnamese children.

That inspired me, and I wanted to hand out more tracts. Two mil-itary units were attached to our headquarters. One was an artillery compound that had twenty soldiers in it. And on the west side of our headquarters was an infantry unit of about 120. I thought, "There are still several hours in the light of day." Being emboldened by the exam-ple set by the children, I collected a box and started out the gate over to the compound. Sure enough, Biet Nungh had fifteen kids lined up behind me. I gave them all handfuls of the gospel of John.

At the artillery compound, I went up to the guard and indicated that I wanted to go in. He said, "Sure, but the kids cannot come in." Well, that thwarted my plan for handing out the tracts. Not knowing what else to do, I went in alone. Immediately, I began challenging God. I asked Him, "What are the chances that the kids are still going to be there when I finish making the rounds of these twenty or so soldiers and some family members?"

I did that in about twenty-five minutes and walked out of the artillery compound. And sure as my lack of faith affirmed, the kids were gone. I was disappointed but thought, "Well, I'll go over to the large compound and do what little I can." When I walked inside the gate, there were the fifteen children. They had completed as much rapid running of feet as God's little disciples could do. Everyone in that compound—hundreds of people—had the gospel of John in their hands by the time we were finished. Again, God, in His mild, loving rebuke, said, "You know, I can accomplish anything I want to, even though you lack sufficient faith to believe it."

A God-Ordained Mission

Then I became even more motivated because I recognized that God had ordained precisely why I was building this relationship with the children—He wanted to present five thousand copies of the gospel of John to the people in the local villages. The next day and for several days after that, when I would get in the Jeep, mysteriously, the lines of communication wordlessly went out. By the time I got outside the compound, there were fifteen kids in my Jeep. In the daytime, travel was pretty safe. The war was fought at night. So we would go from one village to the next. And in the Asian culture, unlike the New York City subway, if you hand someone a tract, it will make it much farther than the nearest Dumpster.

In the Asian culture, if you hand something to an individual, he or she receives it as a "present." The summary of this story is that I knew that the military mission, the operational mission, was a total failure. But I also knew that five thousand copies of the gospel of John were circulating around Khanh Hoa Province. I pray for the people there constantly, and I always have a desire to go back because I just know there was a witness in that area, perhaps a church and a congregation of believers, as a result of God mobilizing an army, a faithful mother, and a wife who prayed me through harm's way.

Heal Our Heroes

I've been in the nonprofit business for more than fifteen years. My wife and I did a lot of work internationally with Campus Crusade for Christ (now CRU). But when she took ill and her memory started to be affected, we could no longer travel. I am the primary caregiver for her in her advanced stage of Alzheimer's. About five years ago, I started the nonprofit called Heal Our Heroes, and it allows me to work locally. It has been very effective because in this smaller area, we can be more vertical in our ministry. Before, we were an inch deep and a mile wide. We traveled internationally to lead conferences on military bases all over the world.

We try to bring veterans from hopelessness to hope, moving them through the system to the point of being able to reintegrate back into society. Doing that is therapy for my own PTSD. It's a little bit tricky because as I sit around the conversation center, which you probably grew up knowing as a campfire, I have to prime the pump first to get the conversation moving. I do that by relating my past, and the story unfolds as we go forward. But then for a couple of nights after that, I don't sleep, and I have the flashbacks. It triggers episodes that are commonly associated with PTSD. Yet it's also cathartic for me to connect with other veterans who like to know that someone has been where they are.

What Veterans Experience

The military is a culture. It is a group of people just like any other group that needs someone to reach out in a missionary environment, to understand their issues and needs, and walk beside them at the point of knowledge. It clearly is more effective to minister to veterans if you are a veteran.

I will sit around the campfire and look at a veteran who has engaged me conversationally, just casually, and say, "Tom, I know probably four things about you, and I met you just an hour ago over a hot dog and a hamburger. Number one, you're constantly agitated or pissed off. Number two, you probably have trouble sleeping most nights because of images you keep seeing. Number three, you probably picked up an addiction while you were deployed. And number four, there's probably no intimacy in your relationship. You might ask how I know all that, and it's because I have been there. I've been precisely where you are."

My direct challenge, as only one veteran can challenge another, is saying, "Until you're ready to look inside yourself and agree that there's a crisis going on, you will not move forward. You will stay in your man-cave chair with a six-pack and a television remote and stay there forever, unhappy. By the way, how is that working out for you?"

Most veterans have a sense of anger, inadequacy, and failure, as well as a complete loss of significance when they are no longer in active duty. When you take away their uniform, their unit, and their mission, you have sucked 99 percent of the significance out of their lives. That's why suicide often becomes an option. Although the statistics say that 23 to 27 percent of soldiers come back from combat with PTSD, the Veterans Administration and others say that all veterans are affected by combat deployments to varying degrees. They are all dealing with trauma at various levels.

That's why I'm so driven to tell these veterans that there's no healing without honesty. I tell them, "You need to tell your story, and then together, we can see how your story molds naturally into the greatest story ever told—that of God's grace." Then it becomes one story.

Three Ways Veterans Cope with the Nightmarish Memories

My PTSD did not show up until God called me into vocational ministry at age fifty. When I sold my business and followed God's calling to serve Him, I began to relive my military fears. I began to tell my stories and was able to relate to those in current active duty, whether it was at marriage conferences or trauma conferences, I began to open the closet of my sealed past. And there were my nightmares, my demons, and the images of children from the first night I was in Vietnam. It all hit me like a freight train. I could hear the sounds. I could see the body parts. I could see the triage, the mutilation. All those things came flooding back. I would wake up with cold sweats and feel like I was having a heart attack, and I couldn't breathe. An overwhelming tidal wave of despair washed over me.

That's what happens to so many veterans. They don't dare talk about it or even think about it, because if they do, they don't know what's on the other side of that closet. Veterans deal with that "closet" called their military past in one of three ways. The first type of veteran locks the closet door and never dares to mention a word. The second type of veteran will open the closet door of his past, go in, and close it behind him. He will be consumed by it, and he or she will live under a bridge or in the woods, totally dysfunctional and unable to live in a normal society.

The third type of veteran is able to open that door and leave it open. Typically with someone else's support, he or she will enter cautiously, judiciously, into the past and begin to unbundle what he or she experienced, walk it back, tone it down, and gain the perspective that only God can take a life. No life can be taken without God's hand. We are not God. Once I can get a veteran to this point, then I can walk him or her through the issues.

Working with veterans is how I pay God's grace forward. My trauma has not gone away, but it is tempered and has become manageable. I must get this message to other veterans. I must give them hope because I have been through that feeling of hopelessness. It doesn't go away.

When I came home from Vietnam, I brought a bronze star for valor with me. I thought that was all I had brought home, but I didn't realize for almost thirty years that I also brought the war home. It took over my life. It was devastating. It made me angry. It made me hypervigilant, and I didn't want people around me. I didn't want to hear sounds and smells that became emotional barrages that took me back to those images and those places. But by God's grace, and by His Word, just like with grieving, God's grace began to pull me through, and I began to regain my perspective.

Our organization is founded on the premise that we are mind, body, and spirit. The military will recognize only the mind and the body, but not the spirit. I say to those we work with that in the spirit of a man or a woman is where your chaplain would tell you faith and hope reside and where your mind can be renewed. Your mind can be transformed through a relationship with the God who heals, Jehovah Rapha. Our purpose is to honor and heal the veterans in our area and assist them in getting hired.

Modeling God's Grace

When my wife and I worked at a conference center, I simply introduced us like this: "I'm Bob, and this is my wife, Sam. We have three sons. One is in college, one is a senior in high school, and our third son went home to be with the Lord when he was seven, when he was tragically run over by a neighbor." The moment we would say that, many people wanted to speak with us because they were feeling a crushing sense of loss too, whether it was because of a miscarriage, the death of a sibling, or the death of a spouse. They would say, "I just need to talk to you." We didn't realize that God would place us in a ministry for those who grieve.

Yet it took being bereaved parents to do that. Around the time Michael was killed, God called us from marriage conferencing into a conference center, where people were coming through constantly. We were able to pay God's grace forward in the lives of military families again, for those who had lost their husbands or fathers in combat.

During our seven-year conference-center ministry, we paid forward the enabling grace that we received through Michael's death to others who found themselves swimming in an ocean of hurt, grief, despair, and even anger at God. We helped them move through that, get another perspective, and appropriate God's grace in their lives. God blessed our lives for His glory by having us minister to other people.

Learning What God Wants

As a kid, I went to Sunday school and church every time it was open, and to my parents' credit, I probably memorized hundreds of Bible verses. I still have most of them. I forget a lot of things, but I don't forget those Bible verses.

For me, there is a difference between being saved and having a relationship with God. I grew up believing we were in control of our salvation. We believed that if we sinned, we could lose our salvation. So I got saved every summer, and I got saved every Friday night when I was dating—I had to pray again. But when I met my wife, Sam, I fell in love. I was totally captivated by her. I wanted to share everything with her. She was in Bible college, and she received the most demerits of the year as a freshman because I would not get off the phone with her. She missed every curfew because I was so captivated by her.

When I was on active duty, a commissioned officer going to intel school in Washington, DC, I dropped Sam off one day, and then God's voice filled my car. He said, "Bob, *that's* what I want—I just want you to share your life with me like you do with Sam. I want you to tell me what you're thinking. I want you to tell me what you want and what you need. I just want you to fall in love with me, let me walk with you, and let me share life with you." It came on like a burst of Fourth of July fireworks. I realized, "This is it. It's not about maintaining rules; it's not about sinning. It's not about having guy thoughts. God wants me to have a *relationship* with Him, just like I have a relationship with Sam!" Oh, was I set free. That happened before I got married at twenty-one years old, which is when I think my true salvation took place.

That changed everything. Then the Bible made sense. All the verses made sense because they were birthed out of a relationship, not out of rules and laws. Once you enter that relationship, you're empowered to walk with God and seek His approval through obedience. If we love Him, we will obey Him. That became doable in the power of the Holy Spirit, and it was very transforming in terms of my testimony.

Psalm 91 is the Scripture Bob has relied on the most. He calls on a number of verses in this passage of Scripture almost daily. He said it is the soldier's psalm, and he has given copies of it to hundreds of veterans:

> Whoever dwells in the shelter of the Most High will rest in the shadow of the Almighty. I will say of the LORD, "He is my refuge and my fortress, my God, in whom I trust." Surely he will save you from the fowler's snare and from the deadly pestilence. He will cover you with his feathers, and under his wings you will find refuge; his faithfulness will be your shield and rampart. You will not fear the terror of night, nor the arrow that flies by day, nor the pestilence that stalks in the darkness, nor the plague that destroys at midday. A thousand may fall at your side, ten thousand at your right hand, but it will not come near you. You will only observe with your eyes and see the punishment of the wicked. If you say, "The LORD is my refuge," and you make the Most High your dwelling, no harm will overtake you, no disaster will come near your tent. For he will command his angels concerning you to guard you in all your ways; they will lift you up in their hands, so that you will not strike your foot against a stone. You will tread on the lion and the cobra; you will trample the great lion and the serpent. "Because he loves me," says the Lord, "I will rescue him; I will protect him, for he acknowledges my name. He will call on me, and I will answer him; I will be with him in trouble, I will deliver him and honor him. With long life I will satisfy him and show him my salvation." (Psalm 91:1–16)

There are some verses in Psalm 121 that Bob calls on too. His seven-year-old son, Michael, had been memorizing Psalm 121:1–2 the week before he was killed: "I lift up my eyes to the mountains—where does my help come from? My help comes from the LORD, the Maker of heaven and earth" (Psalm 121:1–2).

My Thoughts on Bob's Story

I know it must take great courage for Bob to share the horrific experiences he witnessed in Vietnam, because doing so causes him to relive them. Through his courage, he leads other veterans to face their own nightmarish memories with courage too.

Bob's mother sounds like a wonderful, faithful woman who gave her son a solid foundation of faith from the beginning of his life, and she modeled a godly life for him to follow. It was fortunate that Bob had that faith to turn to during his tour of duty, as well as the prayers of his mother and his wife during that difficult time.

It also took great faith for Bob to leave a thriving business to follow God's call into vocational ministry. He and his wife provide valuable support to hundreds of veterans and their families and to grieving parents who have lost a child. Now Bob is a pillar of support to the veterans in his community, and he views that service as his way of paying God's grace forward. He also finds relief from his own PTSD in the nonprofit foundation he established for veterans. Bob serves as a wonderful example for all of us in following His call to serve the Lord in a way that aligns with our unique God-given experiences and talents.

Time for Personal Reflection

1. Bob said the Bible finally made sense to him once he realized that God wanted a relationship with him. He says it's not about following rules and laws. Instead, "Once you enter that relationship, you're empowered to walk with God and seek His approval through obedience." To what extent do you focus on your relationship with God, as opposed to following commandments and rules you think you are expected to follow?

2. Bob tells veterans, "You need to tell your story, and then together, we can see how your story molds naturally into the greatest story ever told—that of God's grace." To what extent are you able to link your most difficult experiences to the story of God's grace? Spiritual sharing can not only lead to personal healing but it can also positively impact the lives of all those who hear your story.

Finding Strength in Weakness: How Cancer Saved My Life

In September 2016, Karen served as the USA flag bearer at the World Triathlon/ Aquathlon Championships in Cozumel, Mexico. She placed fourth in her age division just four months after being immobilized by tumors in her spine and pelvis.

This story is about Karen Newman, who survived stage III breast cancer and is now battling an aggressive form of metastatic stage IV breast cancer. Here are some statistics about breast cancer from the nonprofit organization Breastcancer.org:

Breast cancer incidence rates in the United States began decreasing in 2000, after increasing for the previous two decades. They dropped by 7% from 2002 to 2003 alone, possibly because of women's reduced use of hormone replacement therapy (HRT) after the results of a large study called the Women's Health Initiative were published in 2002. These results suggested a connection between HRT and increased breast cancer risk. These decreases are [also] thought to be the result of treatment advances, earlier detection through screening, and increased awareness. ...

Besides skin cancer, breast cancer is the most commonly diagnosed cancer among American women. In 2017, it's estimated that about 30% of newly diagnosed cancers in women will be breast cancers. ...

As of March 2017, there are more than 3.1 million women with a history of breast cancer in the United States. This includes women currently being treated and women who have finished treatment.[6]

The most advanced-stage breast cancers are those that are recurrent and metastatic:

Recurrent breast cancer is breast cancer that comes back after a period of time, often because it was not detected in initial testing. The cancer may come back in the same or opposite breast or chest wall.

Metastatic breast cancer is breast cancer that has spread to another part of the body. Cancer cells can break away from the original tumor in the breast and travel to other parts of the body through the bloodstream or the lymphatic system.[7]

The severity of an individual's cancer prognosis is based on the internal progression of the disease. As Breastcancer.org explains, oncologists take many factors into consideration when they diagnose a patient as having a particular "stage" of cancer:

The stage of cancer is usually expressed as a number on a scale of 0 through IV, with stage 0 describing non-invasive cancers that remain within their original location and stage IV describing invasive cancers that have spread outside the breast to other parts of the body. ... Cancer stage is based on four characteristics: the size of the cancer, whether it is invasive or non-invasive, whether cancer is in the lymph nodes, [and] whether it has spread to other parts of the body beyond the breast. ... [For example,] stage IV describes invasive breast cancer that has spread beyond the breast and nearby lymph nodes to other organs of the body, such as the lungs, distant lymph nodes, skin, bones, liver, or brain.[8]

Karen is an award-winning triathlete, inspirational speaker, dietitian, wife, mother of three sons, and author. She is working on her second book. She suffered from low self-esteem when she was a girl and forty years of eating disorders that almost killed her, partly as the result of bullying. Her positive attitude in the midst of those crises and her battle with cancer is a gift and an inspiration to many, including me.

Her first book, *Just Three Words,* has brought hope to many people who are facing fear and an uncertain future because of a medical diagnosis. She has started a "God group," which she describes as "a safe place where everyone is welcome to come, be blessed, pray, and share stories of brokenness and victory."

Here is Karen's story.

It would be easy to begin by telling you all the glossy, wonderful words that have been used to describe me and my successes, but that just doesn't feel authentic. I've spent too many years hiding, striving, and pretending to be someone I thought everyone wanted me to be. Instead I wound up lost, lonely, in the throes of an addiction, and nearly dead.

I want this story to inspire everyone to know that we can truly thrive only when we open ourselves to love and have the courage to fully embrace who we really are.

So on that note, here is my real story.

Bullying and Its Resulting Pain

On my first day of middle school, the bullying began. Up until that point, no one had ever called me a name or made fun of me. My kind and loving parents held my two brothers and me to high standards. Hurting others was simply out of the question. But that rule

After the 2008 Westchester Triathlon in Rye, New York. Karen (in front) with her family: husband Peter (behind) and sons (left to right) Stetson, Chase, and Trent.

didn't apply to the outside world, and I quickly learned what it was like to feel pain and shame. The insults started with my long nose and quickly moved on to other body parts, and then to who I was.

For years, my tormentor and her cohorts glowed with power as I sank deeper. Their daily abuse penetrated my life and took the magic out of it, and I wasn't the same after that. In a desperate attempt to change my circumstances, I reached for the unattainable: perfection. I thought if I volunteered more, worked harder to compensate for my dyslexia, and looked or behaved a certain way, that God, my parents—everyone—would love and accept me. And then my life would matter.

But it didn't work. Instead it left me cloaked in shame and feeling worthless because I couldn't possibly measure up. It was hard not to believe all the lies I heard and felt about myself. I cultivated them until they became an unruly garden in my mind. I forgot every positive thing about myself. Like how I naturally made people happy, never gave up on a challenge, and earned the nickname "Speedy" by running and racing against everyone (and almost always winning). I forgot how the gift of running made me grateful for the great big, gorgeous world that God created. I completely lost sight of the fact that my parents and God loved me unconditionally. There was no more me—only me trying to be the person I thought everyone wanted me to be.

In the dark haze that engulfed me, I spiraled out of control. I became anorexic at the age of fourteen, almost killed myself with starvation in high school, and then discovered bulimia in college. The addiction tormented me for nearly forty years.

Blessed—But Not without Struggles

In the midst of my suffering, I became a registered dietitian and nutritionist, earning a master's degree in clinical nutrition.

The intrigue with the subject of food—and becoming a professional in the field—is not at all surprising given my trials. More information gave me more control. I was a sponge. I learned everything I could and loved helping others overcome and thrive in my private nutritional consulting practice. But inside, my own demons roared, and the secrets flourished. I knew I was living a lie and was a hypocrite.

Karen, who had undergone eleven chemotherapy treatments, gave her testimony after competing and coming in fourth at the Westchester Triathlon, qualifying her to compete at the National Triathlon Championships. The *Today* show filmed the race (youtube.com/watch?v=SW8C_pn9mf0).

Amazingly, despite my eating disorder, the shame that cloaked me daily, and my inability to truly love myself, I somehow managed to attract and fall in love with my college sweetheart, Peter. I married him six years after graduating from the University of Vermont. I hid most of my secrets even from him.

We longed for children, but I wasn't sure if it was possible, given the years of damage my body had endured. But miraculously, God blessed us with three beautiful boys: Stetson, Chase, and Trent. I was overjoyed to be a mother, but unfortunately, despite this incredible gift, the bulimic demon remained. On and off it continued its torture in my mind, body, and spirit. Consulting, running, the new-found sport of triathlon—and my increasing prowess in it—were some of the few successes that buoyed me and kept me going.

In 2000, at the age of thirty-nine, I qualified for Team USA and was invited to compete at the Age-Group World Triathlon Championships in Edmonton, Canada. As I marched to the start of my first World Championship after donning my USA uniform, I cried with pride. Since then, I've raced all over the world, become a coach, earned the title "All-American Triathlete" seven times, stood on numerous podiums, and even broke a world record in my age group.

Triathlon helped me beat away the negative voices in my head. But unfortunately, triathlon wasn't enough.

The Odd Blessing of Cancer

At age forty-six, I was in the worst throes of my bulimia addiction. I'd hit rock bottom and was begging God to end my life. It didn't happen. Instead, just a few weeks later, He threw me a lifeline when I was diagnosed with advanced, stage III breast cancer. The words, "Karen, it's cancer," completely changed my life. Those three words ignited a spark inside and helped me step out of the darkness and into the light. Although I went through chemo, radiation, multiple surgeries, lymphedema, and several other setbacks, I can absolutely say that experiencing cancer was a blessing in my life because of how I was transformed and what I learned from it. And I never stopped training and racing, through it all.

I had made a promise to our boys on that fateful day—March 18th, 2008—that I would fight the cancer and continue to race for my country in my beloved sport. I would show the world that I was strong—a warrior. Triathlon was my metaphor for life ... for overcoming adversity and getting to the finish line. And miraculously, I came back to win more than I ever had before ... in triathlon and in life.

Karen was the keynote speaker at a Center for Hope luncheon in May 2016, just a few days before she collapsed and was taken to the ER, where doctors discovered a tumor in her spine and pelvis.

I've learned that God is all-powerful and all-loving and that He has an incredible plan for our lives. Trials are often opportunities to grow and transform. Just look around, and you will find the blessings. Miracles really do happen, prayers work, and each of us matters. You matter. There will never be another you. Embrace who you are—a magnificent creation. Perfectly imperfect.

Today, I stand in the glorious light of love, redemption, and hope. I'm now an inspirational speaker, an author, a world-record-breaking triathlete, a survivor of two life-threatening diseases, and a woman who has finally found love for herself.

I've been featured on NBC's *TODAY Show* twice, as well as on ABC, and have received multiple awards, all of which bring me to tears of gratitude and awe. Just a few of the awards I have received include USA Triathlon's Most Inspirational Comeback Award, the Connecticut Sports Writers' Alliance's Courage Award, and being named the American Cancer Society's DetermiNation Champion.

Karen poses with her medals before donating them to medals 4mettle.org. She said, "It was a turning point in my life when I realized that my medals didn't dictate my worth and that by giving them away, I could bless many."

From the Pit, Not the Pedestal

My life's journey from near death to life is so powerful and so miraculous that I, with the help of my wonderful cousin and editor, Nancy Burcham, wrote a book called *Just Three Words*. It was not in my power, but in God's. He recruited me, a dyslexic, bullied, loved survivor, and it took three years to write.

The God-breathed book that I never planned on writing is healing a nation. The emails, texts, calls, and online posts of the multiple ways the book is transforming people's lives makes my heart sing. What a gift! It has opened doors for me to give sermons in churches and become an inspirational speaker, allowing me more opportunities to help others find freedom, love, and victory in their own lives. It makes every challenge I have ever faced worth it because I come from a place of being there too. God truly is the Magnificent Father who changes ordinary water into extraordinary wine.

His grace, love, and mercy inspired me to start a God group—a safe place where everyone is welcome to come, be blessed, pray, and share stories of brokenness and victory. And blessedly, my eyes have now been opened to witness firsthand the miraculous hand of Jesus at work.

My prayer is that my story inspires you through your own trials and helps you realize that you are worthy, loved, and vital here on earth. And that you are never too far away or too broken to be healed. You, too, can *live victorious, loved, and free.*

When asked to select a few Bible verses that provided her with strength and comfort during the times when she struggled the most, Karen found it hard to narrow the list down. She chose the following as a sampling of her favorites:

> Be strong and courageous. Do not be afraid or terrified because of them, for the LORD your God goes with you; he will never leave you nor forsake you. (Deuteronomy 31:6)

> He performs wonders that cannot be fathomed, miracles that cannot be counted. (Job 5:9)

> But those who hope in the LORD will renew their strength. They will soar on wings like eagles; they will run and not grow weary, they will walk and not be faint. (Isaiah 40:31)

My Thoughts on Karen's Story

A cancer diagnosis plummets many people into an abyss of depression and despair; they give up all hope and assume their lives are over. But the opposite happened when Karen was diagnosed with cancer—she realized that her life was worth fighting for. Karen battled childhood bullying, a decades-long eating disorder, and chronic self-esteem issues. But out of those crises, she found the courage and conviction to love herself and accept God's grace, acknowledging that "trials are often opportunities to grow and transform."

She also realizes that the trials in her life have uniquely equipped her to lead others to experience God's grace. They have allowed her "more opportunities to help others find freedom, love, and victory in their own lives." Karen's story is a testament to the fact that times of crisis reveal the true nature of our faith—not to God, because He already knows how faithful we are—but to us. Karen wants to share her website so she can help as many people as possible. To read more about her, her book, or simply to be inspired, please visit thekarennewman.com.

Time for Personal Reflection

1. Karen says cancer saved her life. That might sound like a contradiction to some, but if you have been through a similar situation, maybe you can relate to that statement. Have you ever endured a hardship in life that was so challenging that it led you to lean on God and realize that He is the one who could deliver you from the pain? If so, how did that experience change you?

2. When speaking to and inspiring others, Karen says about cancer, "It makes every challenge I have ever faced worth it because I come from a place of being there too." To what extent do you think God uses our deliverance from personal difficulties to show others the endless grace He pours out on His children? If you have had glimpses of God's grace, like Karen, you will be enriched and blessed by sharing those stories with others.

Healed in Body and Spirit

Joe Minarik.

The next story is about Joe Minarik, who battled an aortic aneurysm and kidney failure. God healed both life-threatening conditions and restored Joe's health—and his faith.

According to WebMD, an aortic aneurysm is "a bulge in a section of the aorta, the body's main artery. The aorta carries oxygen-rich blood from the heart to the rest of the body. Because the section of the artery with the aneurysm is overstretched and weak, it can burst. If the aorta bursts, it can cause serious bleeding that can quickly lead to death."[9]

WebMD goes on to explain that "aneurysms can form in any section of the aorta, but they are most common in the belly area (abdominal aortic aneurysm). They can also appear in the upper body (thoracic aortic aneurysm). Medical problems such as high blood pressure and atherosclerosis (hardening of the arteries), weaken the artery walls. These problems, along with the wear and tear that naturally occurs with aging, can result in a weak aortic wall that bulges outward."[10]

Likewise, kidney disease can also exacerbate or cause high blood pressure and heart problems, in addition to other health concerns, as The National Kidney Foundation explains:

> *Chronic kidney disease* includes conditions that damage your kidneys and decrease their ability to keep you healthy … If kidney disease gets worse, waste can build up in the blood and make the patient feel sick. He or she may develop complications like high blood pressure, anemia (low blood count), weak bones, poor nutritional health and nerve damage. Also, kidney disease increases the risk of having heart and blood vessel disease. Chronic kidney disease may be caused by diabetes, high blood pressure and other disorders. Early detection and treatment can often keep chronic kidney disease from getting worse. When kidney disease progresses, it may eventually lead to kidney failure, which requires dialysis or a kidney transplant to maintain life.[11]

Statistics recorded by the National Kidney Foundation indicate that "30 million American adults have CKD [chronic kidney disease], and millions of others are at increased risk. … Heart disease is the major cause of death for all people with CKD. … [because] hypertension causes CKD, and CKD causes hypertension." The good news is that early detection can help keep kidney disease from progressing to kidney failure. Simple lab tests can detect CKD.[12]

Joe, who is now sixty years old, grew up in New Jersey. When he was eighteen, he and his friends met an angel who saved their lives. But after Joe's beloved grandfather died, Joe lost faith in God. Through a miraculous event that can be explained only as divine intervention, Joe's faith in God was restored. Not long after that, God saved Joe's life again. It took three miracles to restore Joe's faith in God forever. Here is his story, which he wishes to dedicate to his mother and father, Evelyn and Joe Minarik.

Angelic Aid

In 1975, I was eighteen years old. One Friday, I went with my friends, Brian and Lou, to New Gretna in South Jersey to visit a friend. The next day, we were going to go target shooting in an area known as the Pine Barrens. It was in November, and we ran into a snowstorm. At about 11:00 p.m., we were on the last road to get to the home of another friend, Andy, when we ran out of gas. We were stuck on an isolated road for three hours in the biting cold snowstorm. Finally, we saw a truck approaching us. It stopped, and the driver asked if we needed help. I told him we had run out of gas.

"I happen to have five gallons in my truck," he said. He went around to the back of his truck, got a gas can, and filled up our tank with a few gallons of gasoline.

I tried to give him money, but he wouldn't take it. He said, "Please, if you see that someone needs help, stop and help them."

I said, "Sure. I would like to fill this gas can up and return it to you. Do you live around here?"

He said, "Yes, a mile down this road." He told me the street name and number and said to make a right, and it was the third house on the left. He said his name was Frank Gilmore.

The next morning, we put gas in a gas can and drove to take it to him. We knew where we had run out of gas, but we couldn't find the street. In fact, there wasn't any street off that road for miles. So we drove to the police station, and they told us no such street existed in New Gretna or in Forked River, the next town over. We looked at each other and said, "He had to be an angel."

When I got home, I said to my friends, "I will send money to Frank Gilmore in two envelopes—one addressed to New Gretna and one to Forked River." I did so, and a week later, both came back to me, stamped "Undeliverable." That has stayed with me all my life. I always think about it. That experience made me a more caring and giving person.

Losing Faith

My maternal grandfather was Czechoslovakian. We called him Gigi, which means Grandpa, but later on we called him Gid. I was the firstborn, so I was one of his favorites. My brother came along four years later and my sister four years after that. He gave me more money than my brother and sister. He bought a lot of bicycles when I was a kid because if one was a little rusted, he would say, "Hey, we have to buy you a new one."

At the beginning of 1987, I moved to California. Gid visited me when he was eighty-nine years old. We had a great three weeks together. In 1989, he had a tumor removed. He called me a day before the operation and said in his broken English with his Eastern European accent, "I am never going to see you again. I go for big operation. I think I be finished!"

That shook me up. I told him, "I am going to move back to Cape Cod. I am going to sell my house out here."

He said, "Oh, you come back? All right, then, I wait for you because I love you too much."

The operation was successful. I had a year to be with Gid before he started to go downhill. He passed away toward the end of 1990 at the age of ninety-three. After his death, I was mourning him so much that I blamed God for taking him away from me. I lost all confidence in God. "How can you take him from me?" I asked, even though Gid had lived for ninety-three years. I was selfish at the time.

Restored Faith—with a Second Miracle

One night four months later, I awoke at 3:00 a.m., and something told me to go in the living room and get a book from the bookshelf. I tried to turn on a light in the bedroom, but it would not turn on. I walked into the hallway and tried to turn that light on, but it wouldn't turn on, either. The same thing happened in the living room. I made my way to the bookshelf in the dark and pulled out a book; I didn't know which book I had chosen. I found my way to the dining room table. I opened the book I had gotten from the shelf and lay it on the table. In the dark, I made my way to the light switch in the dining room, and the light came on.

So I went back to the table and saw that the book I had taken off the shelf was the Bible. The Scripture I had opened the Bible to in the pitch dark was John, chapter 4:

> Once more he visited Cana in Galilee, where he had turned the water into wine. And there was a certain royal official whose son lay sick at Capernaum. When this man heard that Jesus had arrived in Galilee from Judea, he went to him and begged him to come and heal his son, who was close to death. "Unless you people see signs and wonders," Jesus told him, "you will never believe." The royal official said, "Sir, come down before my child dies." "Go," Jesus replied, "Your son will live." The man took Jesus at his word and departed. While he was still on the way, his servants met him with the news that his boy was living. When he inquired as to the time when his son got better, they said to him, "Yesterday, at one in the afternoon, the fever left him." Then the father realized that this was the exact time at which Jesus had said to him, "Your son will live." So he and all his household believed. (John 4:46–53)

That story hit me hard. Here was a government official who didn't believe in God but needed Him desperately for his son's healing. God poured his grace onto the boy, and he lived. In the end, the official's family believed. That is the moment when I started to have faith in God again.

Life-Threatening Illnesses

One day in 2009, I was at work. I felt a numbing sensation in my left arm and leg. I told my boss I was going home. I walked out to my vehicle, and my grandfather, who had passed away nineteen years earlier, said to me, in his broken English, "Don't go to home; go to hospital." His voice was not in my head; he was talking to me as if he were in the room with me.

"Gid, where are you?" I asked. I was turning around looking for him, but he didn't respond. I got in my vehicle and headed to the hospital. The doctors examined me and said I had experienced an aortic aneurysm. There are no symptoms. You have to get an MRI or a CT scan for a firm diagnosis. If my grandfather hadn't warned me, eventually I would have been dead. The aneurysm measured 4.8 cm; they did not want to operate unless it grew to become 5.2 cm. They watched it for six years and finally said, "Now is the time." So I had the operation.

Two months later, I was out of breath. I would walk twenty-five feet and struggle to breathe. My boss finally said I should get checked out.

"I'll go on Monday," I said.

"No—today," he replied.

So I went and got a blood test. The doctor called as I was driving home. "You are in end-stage renal failure," he said.

I hung up on the doctor because I didn't believe him. How could my kidneys be failing? I had never had any problems with my kidneys before. He called back, and I told the doctor, "I am driving my car, and I am about to pick up some barbecue I ordered at a store. I feel tired, but I am fully functional."

He told me, "Get to a hospital right away. You might not ever enjoy the barbecue."

At that point, I thought God was testing my faith in Him, just like when Job was tested. I would say to Him, "Whatever You send my way, I will never lose faith in You. My faith is stronger than ever."

And He did keep things coming. I had to go on dialysis. One day at the hospital, I told my beautiful fiancée, Karen, "You should bail out now. I don't know what the future holds." When I was having the heart problems—the aortic aneurysm—I had proposed to her, and she had said yes.

She said to me, "Joe, I want to take care of you for the rest of my life."

I asked my mother to pray for me; she was very religious. She said, "I am praying for you—you have no idea how much."

In September of 2015, Karen and I got married.

Meanwhile, my parents' health started to decline. I took them to their doctors' appointments as much as I could; I had to see doctors myself. Even with my health problems, Karen took care of my parents and her mother. Then a lot of things happened within the next six months. My father passed away at the end of December 2015, and my mother passed away three weeks later. Two months later, we got news that Karen could donate a kidney to me; she was a match. Six months after that, my mother-in-law passed away.

My Third Miracle

The kidney transplant was scheduled for July 2016. But it got postponed because someone at the hospital had read a report wrong. So we rescheduled it for August. The transplant got postponed again because I came down with a blood infection. They told me that if I had waited twelve hours longer to see a doctor, I would have been dead. I was in the hospital for two weeks but emerged fine after taking antibiotics. One week after that, I got another blood infection, and we had to clear that up with antibiotics. I was on dialysis at the time, and they checked my blood count. Suddenly, for no apparent reason, it was in the normal range! The doctors took me off dialysis and said, "We'll see what happens; your numbers look good."

It was a miracle! Everything was just fine—the doctors even told me my kidneys were working again. They removed the catheter from my chest, discontinued my dialysis, and told me I did not need a kidney transplant. Was it a miracle from God? You'd better believe it! There is no other way to explain it. You know, if you have faith in God and believe in the power of prayer, anything can happen.

Paying Grace Forward

For a long time, the only people I shared these stories with were my parents because other people either didn't believe things like this can happen, or they thought I made up the stories. It's the same as trying to preach the gospel to someone who doesn't want to hear it. What I usually do is plant a seed in someone's mind in a roundabout way. My mother always told me, "Just plant the seed, Joe. If it takes, then fine." But lately I've given my testimony at church and I've been telling these stories to others, and most people believe them. It is an effective way to bring up the subject of Jesus' love, mercy, and grace with those who don't believe in His miracles yet.

I am so grateful to God for the miracles He has performed in my life, I want to help others in any way I can. I remember the words of the angel God sent to help my friends and me back in 1975, and now I heed them. He said, "Please, if you see that someone needs help, stop and help them." So I do. Small acts of kindness are rewarding and easy to deliver.

Sometimes at the grocery store, someone will be short of money, and they will have a baby with them. They will start to tell the cashier that they will put back some of the items in their cart. I will say, "Oh, no you don't … I will pay for them." There have also been times when older people are short of money when they go to pay for their groceries, or they have forgotten their wallet. I will pay for their groceries. Also, I am always dropping off canned goods and clothing at church thrift stores.

One of the Bible passages that means a lot to me is the Old Testament story about Job. He went through all kinds of turmoil, but he never gave up on God. As a result, God blessed Job richly and gave him a blessed, long life. I feel that He is doing the same for me:

The LORD blessed the latter part of Job's life more than the former part. He had fourteen thousand sheep, six thousand camels, a thousand yoke of oxen and a thousand donkeys. And he also had seven sons and three daughters. … After this, Job lived a hundred and forty years; he saw his children and their children to the fourth generation. (Job 42:12–13, 16)

Another passage I like a lot is from Luke. Ten men who had leprosy asked Jesus to heal them. Only one of those who had been cleansed returned to show his gratitude and praise God for this blessing. This Scripture has inspired me to praise the Lord and share my own story:

As he was going into a village, ten men who had leprosy met him. They stood at a distance and called out in a loud voice, "Jesus, Master, have pity on us!" When he saw them, he said, "Go, show yourselves to the priests." And as they went, they were cleansed. One of them, when he saw he was healed, came back, praising God in a loud voice. He threw himself at Jesus' feet and thanked him—and he was a Samaritan. Jesus asked, "Were not all ten cleansed? Where are the other nine? Has no one returned to give praise to God except this foreigner?" Then he said to him, "Rise and go; your faith has made you well." (Luke 17:12–19)

My Thoughts on Joe's Story

Often, we humans are stubborn. We resist answering God's call for whatever reason. But God is patient and continues to pour His grace into our lives, even when we resist. God gave Joe another year with his grandfather, and He saved Joe's life twice. He even pointed Joe to a hard-hitting passage of Scripture at the moment when he needed it the most.

Quite a few passages in the Bible describe God as "slow to anger" and "abounding in love." One such verse is Psalm 103:8, which says, "The LORD is compassionate and gracious, slow to anger, abounding in love." Sometimes people view God as an angry, dictatorial tyrant who will punish them if they sin. Joe's story is a beautiful example of God's patience and compassion. He continues to "knock" on our hearts until we let Him in. And when we do, as Joe can attest, our lives are filled with joy, well-being, and gratitude.

Time for Personal Reflection

1. Have there been times in your life when your faith in God dwindled or even lapsed? What happened as a result? Did God "punish" you in some way, or did He perform a miracle in your life, like He did in Joe's life, to show you that He was still with you?

2. Hebrews 11:1 says, "Now faith is confidence in what we hope for and assurance about what we do not see." It's not easy to believe in things we cannot see; that's where the well-known term "leap of faith" comes from. Has there been a time in your life when you prayed and hoped for something and believed the Lord would provide it? Did He provide it? If not, continue to trust in His wisdom, His love, and His perfect timing.

"Lord, I Need Your Help": Facing Chronic Pain

Steven Darter.

Chronic physical pain can rob us of the joy of the everyday blessings in our lives. When there is no relief from pain, it becomes more difficult to withstand even the little annoyances in life. Steve Darter knows this all too well. After being healthy and active his entire life, he began experiencing health issues. His pain reached a point of becoming almost unbearable. This is when he turned to God in prayer. Realizing God's grace in a moment of despair gave Steve an epiphany that all of us can learn from.

The Integrative Pain Center of Arizona lists the following as just some of the long-term effects chronic pain can have on an individual:

Chronic pain ... leaves the pained person with a greatly reduced ability to find solutions or workarounds to even relatively mundane problems. ...

Pain wears a person down, draining his or her energy and sapping motivation. [People with chronic pain] sometimes attempt to limit social contact in an effort to reduce stress and to decrease the amount of energy they have to spend reacting to their environment. ...

Recent studies have also shown that chronic pain can actually affect a person's brain chemistry and change the wiring of the nervous system. Cells in the spinal cord and brain of a person with chronic pain, especially in the section of the brain that processes emotion, deteriorate more quickly than normal.[13]

Steve has been my business associate and friend for more than twenty years. He is the author of *Managing Yourself, Managing Others: Learn How to Improve Effectiveness, Productivity, and Work Satisfaction* and *Lessons from Life: Four Keys to Living with More Meaning, Purpose, and Success.* Steve has had a distinguished forty-year career interviewing, assessing, and advising more than five thousand individuals, ranging from troubled teenagers to CEOs.

He also has considerable experience as a guest speaker and facilitator. He was profiled as one of North America's top executive recruiters in the book The New Career Makers. He has an EdS degree in counseling and personnel from the State University of New York (SUNY) at Albany.

At age sixty-eight, Steve is semi-retired. Here is his story, as written in his second book, *Lessons from Life.*

––––––––––

Frustration, anger, and resentment have a way of creeping up and becoming a way of life, ever so slowly, without even realizing that its malignant effect has taken control of emotions and mind. At least that's what happened to me. My forties were a piece of cake, but my fifties brought an onslaught I wasn't ready for.

The door opened wide when illness, and eventually death, took both my parents. I had grown to admire and appreciate their values, sacrifice, and love for each other and their love of family. They had become an important part of my life, and now they were gone. This difficult time was exacerbated by my son, who was causing significant emotional pain as he struggled with his life and growing into manhood. I was working tremendously long hours, which didn't help. It was wearing down my resistance, both physically and emotionally. To keep up the pace, I was living on caffeine, little sleep at night, and naps.

Medical Issues

My body was also falling apart, and the implications went beyond physical pain. Playing sports, always a haven for me, now became a battle. First came heel spurs, literally making me crawl out of bed and then down the steps. It took six months for the pain to retreat. But I continued to play basketball and tennis. Then came a high ankle sprain, and I was sidelined for months.

Then came knee pain, followed by sciatica pain, which became so severe that I could barely drive the car—mostly doing so on cruise control so I could rest my right leg in such a way that the pain was minimized. Sitting was a problem. I often worked standing up. The sciatica pain lasted just short of two years. I gave up playing basketball, continued to play tennis, and began playing more golf. Then arthritis hit my back. I took so much Aleve, Advil, and Excedrin that I developed stomach pains, so the doctor prescribed Arthrotec.

To survive and overcome the back pain, I began each day with forty-five minutes of stretching and core-strengthening exercise, a routine I maintain to this day. Periodically the pain would return, and sometimes it was so severe that my legs would give out and my body would crumble unless I quickly found a place to sit, or something to grab hold of, to steady myself. Then there was posterior tibular tendonitis; even simple walking was painful. It took several years of visits to physicians, physical therapists, and an orthotist and a routine of foot and ankle strengthening exercises to eventually get the pain to cease, but that, too, would return periodically. My tennis playing was greatly restricted.

Then an enlarged prostate led to urinary tract retention and a visit to the emergency room at a hospital. I learned to catheterize myself, a skill that, even in my wildest imagination, I never thought I'd have to learn. I carried a catheter and gel with me all the time, just in case. Two prostate surgeries ended that need. Between those surgeries, my retina tore, and I was sidelined for six weeks.

Following that, I developed iliotibial band syndrome, with pain running from my hip to the knee in my right leg. I added more stretching and strengthening exercises to my morning routine.

At times, I was not all that pleasant to live with. Just ask my wife,

Diane. I was increasingly aware of how I was behaving—and I didn't like it.

I needed to write—was trying to write—about what all this was doing to me and how I reached a place of frustration and resentment, how it was beginning to skew my perceptions, how I was increasingly seeing what was negative, and how it affected the way I looked at life.

Pain, Surgery, Panic and Fear

Then in 2015, as I was working on another edit of my book, shortly after turning sixty-six years of age, the back and sciatica pain returned in such an excruciating way that it made my previous bouts seem mild in comparison. Sleep became impossible. I was prescribed oxycodone, but after taking it, I had an allergic reaction in the middle of the night, causing difficulty with swallowing and breathing. I survived, on my knees, hands clasped in prayer, begging God to help—to give me peace of mind, a calm heart, and the ability to accept. Calmness came. My throat relaxed. Four days later, I received my first epidural, but the pain persisted. Moderation came after a second epidural. If the pain didn't moderate, the neurosurgeon said, the next step was spinal fusion from the T10 vertebra to my pelvis.

One month later, I lost most of the stability in my right foot and ankle, which had the posterior tibular tendonitis problem. I was advised to have surgery to replace a dead tendon with one from my toes and repair another that had torn, reconstruct my heel and midfoot, repair a torn ligament, remove the arthritis from my ankle (which was described as end stage), and fuse the foot and ankle to my leg. Three screws were inserted into my ankle where it met my leg, and two metal plates were grafted into my foot—one to hold my reconstructed heel in place and the other into my midfoot to hold a newly constructed arch.

During recovery from that surgery, I discovered that I am prone to "cast claustrophobia," resulting in a confined feeling and periodic anxiety and panic attacks. This felt like hell. Eating brought on anxiety, as did the simple task of taking a drink, resulting in feeling as if I were going to choke, that my breathing would stop. I lost ten pounds in four weeks. Even the simple joy of watching TV often brought on anxious feelings. Medicine helped, but it was not enough. My mind and emotions lost control; panic overwhelmed. I prayed. That is when I admitted that I was losing the battle with my panic attacks, that nothing I tried was working. I asked God to take over. I put myself into His hands. I asked Him to help me calm down. Relief was short-lived. God was not yet finished with me.

The "cast claustrophobia" gave way to a debilitating nerve pain in my foot. Panic and anxiety returned, joining forces with my intense nerve pain. I prayed:

Dear God, please help me. My foot hurts; I'm in continuous pain. I'm sad, depressed, restless, anxious. I can't sleep. I lay my head down and feel the pain and anxiety. I try mindful breathing and feel the pain and, again, anxiety. I sit up. I move. I'm exhausted from a lack of sleep—so tired—twenty-four hours a day, seven days a week. I can't stop regretting that I elected to have this foot and ankle surgery. I can't walk. If I sit, there is pain. If I lie down, there is pain. There is no relief. It's difficult to find anything to do to busy myself—to distract me. This nerve pain won't stop; it is unrelenting. I am trying to put all this pain, depression, anxiety, sadness, and regret away from the forefront of my mind. I am trying to do things to distract, but the pain and feelings keep returning. I keep praying, reading the Bible, asking for calmness of the heart and mind, asking for a miracle. Lord, I need Your help. I'm afraid I'm not going to make it. I'm afraid there will be no end to this pain, anxiety, and overwhelming regret, sadness, and depression. God, please help me.

When laid up and hurting as I was, there is plenty of time to think and reflect. When my worry, pain, and panic were most severe—most excruciating—I was driven to depths of fear like never before. Not because it was the most painful, but because it was over a long period of time, and I was helpless, thinking it was permanent.

Understanding God's Viewpoint

I read, I fought, I tried what I could. Nothing helped except turning to God again and asking for help. I prayed in tears, at night, all alone, revealed, naked before the Lord, stripped clean of my sense of control. I admitted that I was infinitesimal, not worthy of anything, but knew that God shows mercy. That is when I realized that I thought I believed, but I had not really embraced my belief fully, my faith, my commitment to God, to Christ, and to the Spirit of God that is inside each of us.

Each night in my pain and panic, I read the Bible, devotions, and words of God on the Internet. I sought God's power and love.

I kept repeating, like a mantra, Philippians 4:5-7: "The Lord is near. Do not be anxious about anything, but in everything, by prayer and petition, with thanksgiving, present your requests to God. And the peace of God, which transcends all understanding, will guard your hearts and your minds" (my heart and mind).

I believed that God would help me get through, survive another sleep-deprived night, another day of pain, panic, and anxiety. I would Google phrases like "God, please help me"; "God and mindfulness to help deal with pain, anxiety, and panic"; and "Jesus, help me with my pain."

I realized that I was on the fence—a convenient believer who had constructed a philosophy, a way to get through life. But it didn't work, at least during this time when all else was failing to help. I had to reach out to God with 100 percent of my heart, mind, and soul.

Each night, I fixed in my mind the image of Jesus reaching out, holding my hand, and saying, "Calm down. I'm with you." It was praying, at first for God, for Jesus, not to abandon me. Then I realized that my prayer should be for me not to abandon, not to deny, not to retreat from God, from Jesus.

Then on February 10, 2016, six weeks after this journey of pain and panic began, I stumbled upon a daily devotional by Pastor Rick Warren, in which he emphasized working at my problem from God's viewpoint—to see the bigger picture. He wrote about the apostle

Paul being chained in prison for two years and how, during that time period, Paul wrote most of the New Testament, and how even some of Nero's family became believers.

I had been so very depressed for so long, and then I read Rick Warren's words. They reminded me of what I already knew but had let pain and worry block out. "There is a reason," I had been told many years earlier. But I had to search for it.

Why was God slowing me down? Why did He force me into a place of pain, panic, and anxiety that I felt was unbearable and never going to end? Now I know: God was giving me the opportunity to get closer to Him, to grow spiritually.

It has taken me a long time to understand and accept that all of us are given pain to endure, that suffering tests and educates our will and souls, and that it may seem unfair and unjust, especially when we are given more than the normal dose. But to let pain invade your mind and spirit, to torture your soul, to diminish your faith only makes it worse and gives it a negative power that it was not designed to have.

What Pain Produced

Through my most intense pain and recovery, I have learned to be more patient, accepting, and appreciative, especially of Diane; my children, grandchildren, family, and friends; and the life I have led thus far. I learned that I am not in control, although at times I keep trying to be. This has strengthened my relationship with God—my dependence on Him. God's presence has become stronger in me. I feel that I am in a continual dialogue with Him.

I also have learned to be more empathetic, understanding, and giving to others who are in pain—to pay attention, to not ignore, to reach out, to connect—even if it is only to say, "I understand what you are going through" or "I'm thinking about you" or "I'm wishing you the best" or "I'm saying a prayer for you" or "How are you doing? Are you feeling any better?" or thinking, "How can I help?"—and taking action. I will never "downplay" or "blow off" someone's physical or emotional pain again. I asked God to bring me health so that I can do better with the remainder of my life, contributing and helping others.

I have come to believe that there is a reason for pain to come into our lives: as a mechanism for development of ourselves and our souls—if we remain open to what can be learned—and if we don't allow bitterness and resentment to dominate.

I am not sure how to define God (I don't know if anyone really can with 100 percent certainty), but I do know that He exists, and I feel His presence. I do know that when I am separated from that presence (from God) because of ego, pain, resentment, or disappointment, I become disconnected from who I was designed to be.

Many years ago, shortly after Art Miller hired me to provide outplacement counseling to executives who had lost their jobs, I worked with an executive from Aetna (Mike Anstey), who told me about being a soldier fighting during World War II, "This was not an experience I would have selected, but I would not give up what I learned from that experience for a million dollars." It took Mike a very long time to obtain a new job. He was sixty years old when he began and sixty-two (if I recall correctly) when his job-hunting journey ended. He felt the same about being fired and the long, painful job-hunting process and fear that he might never work again.

This is how I feel about the pain I have endured: I would not choose to have all this pain—any of this pain, especially this most recent pain. But I do believe I am a better person as a result and that I have moved closer to the way God designed me—closer to achieving the purpose of my life and my intended destiny.

At the end of the story in his book, Steve asks his readers two questions:

1. What pains, disappointments, and injustices have you let invade your mind and spirit, perhaps torturing your soul and diminishing your faith?

2. Have your pains, disappointments, and injustices helped you and your soul to grow, develop, and evolve to a better place, to achieve an inner peacefulness, and to become the person you have been designed to be?

The Bible is a welcome source of comfort for people with both physical and emotional pain. Here are just a few encouraging verses to turn to when seeking relief from pain:

Therefore we do not lose heart. Though outwardly we are wasting away, yet inwardly we are being renewed day by day. (2 Corinthians 4:16)

For just as we share abundantly in the sufferings of Christ, so also our comfort abounds through Christ. If we are distressed, it is for your comfort and salvation; if we are comforted, it is for your comfort, which produces in you patient endurance of the same sufferings we suffer. (2 Corinthians 1:5–6)

But rejoice inasmuch as you participate in the sufferings of Christ, so that you may be overjoyed when his glory is revealed. (1 Peter 4:13)

I consider that our present sufferings are not worth comparing with the glory that will be revealed in us. (Romans 8:18)

Resist him, standing firm in the faith, because you know that the family of believers throughout the world is undergoing the same kind of sufferings. And the God of all grace, who called you to his eternal glory in Christ, after you have suffered a little while, will himself restore you and make you strong, firm and steadfast. (1 Peter 5:9–10)

My Thoughts on Steve's Story

In a conversation with Steve, he mentioned that his nerve pain continues, but it is manageable and not nearly as painful as it had been. He views his ongoing nerve pain as a continual reminder to speak with

God. He said he thinks God allowed this to happen because he was not prioritizing properly and not really listening. "God stopped me for a while so I could listen and learn," he concludes. In effect, he has turned a major negative situation into a positive one as a result of God's grace.

Steve says, "I realized that I was on the fence—a convenient believer who had constructed a philosophy, a way to get through life. But it didn't work, at least not during this time when all else was failing to help. I had to reach out to God with 100 percent of my heart, mind, and soul." It can be difficult to find a positive aspect of a personal crisis, but Steve was able to do so. He realized that he was focusing only on the pain and not looking at the "bigger picture." We all can learn from Steve's experience.

Time for Personal Reflection

1. Steve learned that God allows us to endure pain so that He can develop our souls and so that we can understand others' suffering. If you have experienced chronic pain, try to see the situation from God's viewpoint, as Steve did. What do you think He expects you to learn from your experience with pain?

2. What pain, disappointment, and injustice have you let invade your mind and spirit, perhaps torturing your soul and diminishing your faith?

3. To what extent has your pain helped you and your soul grow, develop, and evolve to a better place, achieve an inner peacefulness, and become the person God designed you to be?

Healing Insights

- People often experience physical and emotional pain simultaneously. Emotional pain can exacerbate physical pain, and vice versa. It is important to acknowledge and treat both types of pain.

- As demonstrated by the stories in this chapter, God can make even a life-threatening injury or illness disappear if the patient earnestly, boldly, and confidently prays for healing and renewal.

- Revelation 21:4 says, "He will wipe every tear from their eyes. There will be no more death or mourning or crying or pain, for the old order of things has passed away." When illness surfaces in ourselves or our loved ones, we need to claim the promise of this verse.

A Prayer for Those Struggling with Emotional or Physical Issues

The stories in this chapter are about crises related to a variety of emotional and physical issues. If you are facing any of these debilitating problems, here is a prayer that you can modify to reflect your situation:

Dear God, the source of health and healing, I hand over to You the pain, frustration, and complications associated with my battle with _____. I pray that You will ease my suffering and restore my vitality. I believe in Your ability to perform miracles, and I pray for a miracle in my life.

Please help me take from this difficult situation the value of being patient with others and being compassionate about their situations. Enable me to support anyone else who is enduring a similar situation so that I can serve as a witness to Your healing powers.

In Jesus' name I pray. Amen.

5

❧

LEARNING FROM CAREER-RELATED CHALLENGES

B y the time people are ready to begin their careers, they should have sufficient education and maturity to put youthful indiscretions behind them. But for whatever reasons—environmental or emotional—sometimes individuals resort to less-than-ideal means of making a living. Some people start out in respectable careers but then stray because of peer influences. Others succumb early on to the lure of instant wealth and find themselves mired in greed, corruption, or addiction.

Some people have difficulty finding vocations they enjoy that make use of their unique talents. God wants people to be happy in their work. Ecclesiastes 3:12–13 says, "I know that there is nothing better for people than to be happy and to do good while they live. That each of them may eat and drink, and find satisfaction in all their toil—this is the gift of God." If you are uncertain about the type of work you will find fulfilling, turn to God in prayer. Ask Him to lead you to a career you will excel in and enjoy, one that will enable you to make a positive difference.

God wants everything you do in life, including your work, to glorify Him. Colossians 3:17 says, "And whatever you do, whether in word or deed, do it all in the name of the Lord Jesus, giving thanks to God the Father through him."

In this chapter are stories about two types of crises that can cause problems during the career-building years: being tempted to commit fraud in the workplace and losing interest in a once fulfilling, successful career due to overwhelming stress.

A few years ago, the leadership development firm Zenger Folkman conducted a study of approximately 20,000 corporate leaders, mostly in North America. They noted that the number and magnitude of incidents of unethical behavior on the part of corporate executives "exceed anything witnessed in prior decades" and that ethical lapses occur mostly among senior executives as opposed to mid-level managers. The reasons for this trend include more pressure being placed on senior executives to produce continual improvement and less oversight of top-level executives.[1]

Another reason executives sometimes suffer ethical lapses is because of what the researchers call "the slippery slope phenomenon." This means people often take a small step in an unethical direction, fully intending to make it right at some point and get back on the right path. "But, once on this slippery slope, it becomes extremely difficult to hop off," the researchers noted. They propose that one solution to the problem is to balance a drive for results with "an equally strong message regarding the methods that are acceptable for attaining those results."[2]

A 2011 report from the nonprofit, nonpartisan Ethics Research Center predicted a surge in unethical behavior among executives. The reasons the researchers gave for this rise in unethical behavior are a bit surprising: a strong economy and the pressure social media puts on people to do things they might not otherwise do.[3]

The report notes that when the economy is sluggish, people are worried about their job security. But when the economy rallies, workers get more comfortable about their futures, and misconduct tends to rise. This is because "profit takes precedence over proper behavior." Also in a strong economy, reporting of misconduct declines, and pressure to compromise increases.[4]

As for the influence of social media on ethics, "the researchers were surprised to find the large role played by active social networkers, defined as those who spend at least 30 percent of their work day partici-pating on social-networking sites." The study revealed that "active social networkers are much more likely to experience pressure to compromise ethics standards and to experience retaliation for reporting misconduct than coworkers who are less involved with social networking."[5]

These negative influences permeate our political, corporate, and social culture. People who think they would never do something unethical sometimes find themselves immersed in scandals they can-not get out of easily.

Here are some Bible verses that can provide a source of comfort to those who are experiencing career-related crises:

> May the favor of the Lord our God rest on us; establish the work of our hands for us—yes, establish the work of our hands. (Psalm 90:17)

> Commit to the Lord whatever you do, and he will establish your plans. (Proverbs 16:3)

> Whatever you do, work at it with all your heart, as working for the Lord, not for human masters. (Colossians 3:23)

Journey of Redemption: From Fraud to Faith

Sometimes, ascending rapidly up the ladder of career success pres-

ents people with temptations that are difficult to overcome. Here, Mark Faris describes how he lost his moral compass and fell prey to the temptations of personal gain from less-than-ethical business practices. Mark was convicted of money laundering, mail fraud, and wire fraud. He was incarcerated in a federal prison and separated from his fam-ily and friends. Cate Greenway, his guardian

Mark Faris.

angel, led him back to making faith, love, and service to God the highest priorities in his life. In 2012, Mark published his memoir, *The Wishing Well.*

Mark was a sales director and later a vice president at a company named Interlink, which sold refurbished networking equipment to larger companies with multiple locations and complex technology requirements. Interlink experienced rapid growth until the tech bubble burst in the early 2000s. To make up for lost revenue, Mark's team began to send false warranty claims to Cisco Systems, requesting newer parts the company knew had high commercial demand. Then they sold the parts and kept the profits. The fraud ultimately cost Cisco Systems about $490,000 and led to the arrest of several Interlink executives. Mark pleaded guilty to charges related to the scheme and spent nearly nine months at a federal prison in Duluth, Minnesota, and another two months in a Minneapolis halfway house.

After being released in 2010, Mark launched MPV Ethics, a training and consulting firm. He speaks to business groups and students about his experience, emphasizing that before you can have *business* ethics, you must have *personal* ethics.

I first met Mark at a business meeting five years ago, He spoke to an audience of more than two thousand people to courageously relate his remarkable story. The audience was mesmerized by his willingness to share his own transgressions and the need for establishing a faith-based moral compass. God's grace, as manifested through Mark's guardian angel, truly transformed his life and empowered him to positively impact the lives of thousands of others.

Here is Mark's story.

I have heard God call me a number of times in my life. In my case, I encountered an angel at the age of fourteen who lived several miles from my home in suburban Kansas City in 1971. I didn't know Cate was an angel at first. Located on her massive pasture and farm was a real wishing well where she prayed to the Lord. Cate would later describe it as her sanctuary.

As my friends and I got to know Cate better, we could see her extensive involvement and philanthropic efforts in our community. She was unlike anyone I had ever met, other than my mother, and she was a surrogate mother to me in many ways.

My family moved to Minneapolis one year later, and I wrote to Cate regularly. She wrote beautiful letters back to me, encouraging me in all aspects of life, particularly my faith in God. I was a wobbly young Catholic boy on most days.

When her letters stopped, I wondered what had happened to Cate. In December 1973, one of her daughters wrote me the following abbreviated letter:

Dear Mark,

Please accept my apologies for not writing you sooner. I am late in writing, and there is a reason for that.

It is with great sadness to report to you that my beloved mother, your friend Cate, suddenly passed away. For several months now, my sister and I have been diligently working to get our affairs with the farm in order and respond to the overwhelming letters and well wishes from the community. You simply cannot fathom how much she was loved and respected by people of all ages. We have all lost our angel, and I miss her so much.

You should also know that we found your letters in a box labeled "The Gang." In it are other letters, pictures, and notes from your friends Maureen, Cindy, and David. Also in Mom's box was a note with your names on it. There is a passage from her that I wish to leave with you: "Lord, thank You for their friendship and love, and never forget our young white doves." Mark, you take care of yourself and your family. We will one day see our angel again.

With warmest regards,
Nina Greenway Wright

My Guardian Angel

After Cate's death, I saw her in a hospital chapel after a traumatic car accident I was involved in where an elderly woman was seriously hurt. She was simply beautiful and perfect in every way. Nothing had changed since the first day I had met her.

After a minute or two, I said, "Mrs. Greenway, I've missed you so much. You must have entered heaven, but why did you leave the planet at an early age?"

Mrs. Greenway replied, "Mark, I bring you good news. Edna will survive and be your friend. Comfort her and Mr. Gustafson. Continue to spend time with them, and everything will work out. You need not worry about things moving forward, as the Lord will manage everything. Maintain your faith, belief, and trust in Him to do the right thing. I must go now. Never forget me. I love you."

I heard her soothing voice a number of times after that, always during crises and trying times in my life.

On August 1, 2009, my second day in a federal prison, I discovered a wishing well by our mess hall. It was too surreal, and I was broken down emotionally, having said good-bye to my family the day before. I stared at the well and heard Cate's wonderful voice. She said, "Your time is now. God has sent me, and He is waiting for you in the chapel."

Moments later, I dropped to my knees and asked God for His love, forgiveness, guidance, and a restart. For 318 days in a row, I started my day off with the Lord to keep me on track.

I have always felt Cate's presence near me. She has never confronted me but always encouraged and guided me to stay on track with God.

The second time I saw Cate after her death was on the morning of April 13, 2010, when I was released from prison. I was kneeling at the wishing well, deep in thought and prayer. I had helped many at the prison camp, and this was the beginning of a foundation that could be expanded. With tears of sorrow and joy, I thanked God, Lord Jesus, the Virgin Mary, the Holy Spirit, and Cate for letting me leave this horrible place.

Guided from Beyond

I slowly opened my eyes, and there was Cate, standing no more than ten feet away, unchanged and still as beautiful as the first day we met, smiling at me. Her glow, sanctity, purity, and light were unmistakable. Unwilling to move and still kneeling, I acknowledged my angel by nodding. Then she spoke. Her words transformed me forever:

> It is time for you to go and reunite with your family. You have traveled a long way in your quest to find your faith, and it all began with my wishing well. It is appropriate that your new journey start with this wishing well and carry you forward to your rightful and permanent home.
>
> Remember what you are saved for—that the Son of God might be manifested in your mortal flesh. Bend the energy of your powers to realize your new election as a child of God; rise to the occasion every time. You cannot do anything for your salvation, but you must do something to manifest it. You must work out what God has worked in. Work it out with your brain, your heart, and your soul. Do not be set in your old ways, for then it is a lie to say God has saved and sanctified you.
>
> Mark, God is the Master Engineer, and he allows the difficulties to come in order to see if you can vault over them properly. Rise to the occasion, and always do the right thing. It does not matter how it hurts as long as it gives God the chance to manifest Himself in your mortal flesh. May the Lord be with you every day of your life and for all eternity. Contribute to the betterment and well-being of your fellow men and women. Always know that I am close by, watching you on God's chosen path. I love you.

My Personal Reflection

After I was arrested in my office on March 14, 2007 and formally arraigned later that day in federal court, I knew my life had changed forever. Would my relationship with my wife, my two boys, eleven and eight years of age, our families, and friends change? What would I say to members of my church and volunteer organizations that were part of my life? Would my reputation be damaged for a while, or was there a chance of restoring it? Would I fight the charges or have the moral courage to admit my guilt?

For the next fifteen months, I dug my heels in and vowed to fight. I was still arrogant, defiant, closed-minded, and unwilling to confront the truth about the fraud I had supported and largely ignored as a company officer. My family and I lived in fear, uncertainty, and doubt. My dialogue with God was self-serving, unrepentant, and unauthentic.

Confronted with substantial evidence pointing to my wrongdoing, personal torment, and significant guilt, I decided to tell the truth and cooperate with federal prosecutors. Failure to do so at the time could have resulted in potential prison time of thirty-six months with substantial fines and restitution.

Separation from my family, friends, and society for three years was incomprehensible and unfathomable. In advance of my formal sentencing on July 1, 2009, I believe that my relationship with God grew considerably; we had honest, raw, and pure dialogue. I knew I had to be punished for my crimes, suffer the consequences of poor behavior, and deploy the lessons learned.

Like all sinners and flawed humans, I have my wobbly days, faith- and direction-wise. My career has never recovered, yet I fight the good fight trying to do my best and serve Him.

The purpose of writing my memoir, *The Wishing Well*, was to thank God, Jesus, and Cate, and also to acknowledge my faith and love for them as my highest priority. They never gave up on me, and this is a reminder that there is hope and salvation for all of us.

Since I returned home more than seven years ago, I have made it my mission to write and speak to various audiences about the importance of building moral compasses and creating values-based cultures that contribute to the improvement of human life.

I talk about avoiding shortcuts and tell people that rationalizing and justifying them leads to slippery slopes that any of us can find. We are all responsible and accountable for our conduct. Without sounding evangelical, I also convey that faith in God is the most important facet of my moral compass, and without Him in close proximity to me, I am nothing but a wandering nomad without purpose or calling.

Mark says the following verses were and still remain instrumental to his well-being and connection to God.

Scripture about Needless Worry:

Therefore I tell you, do not worry about your life, what you will eat or drink; or about your body, what you will wear. Is not life more than food, and the body more than clothes? Look at the birds of the air; they do not sow or reap or store away in barns, and yet your heavenly Father feeds them. Are you not much more valuable than they? Can any one of you by worrying add a single hour to your life? (Matthew 6:25–27)

Scripture about Hope:

Through whom we have gained access by faith into this grace in which we now stand. And we boast in the hope of the glory of God. Not only so, but we also glory in our sufferings, because we know that suffering produces perseverance; perseverance, character; and character, hope. And hope does not put us to shame, because God's love has been poured out into our hearts through the Holy Spirit, who has been given to us. (Romans 5:2–5)

Scripture about Faith:

Then Jesus declared, "I am the bread of life. Whoever comes to me will never go hungry, and whoever believes in me will never be thirsty." (John 6:35)

My Thoughts on Mark's Story

Sometimes when we think of people in prison, we picture hardened criminals who have lived their lives on the streets, in the fast lane, amid drugs and other nefarious activity. Mark does not fit that profile; he came from a good home and had a successful career. His story shows people of faith that by failing to follow the path God has set before them, they can all too easily slide down that "slippery slope." It can be as simple as turning a blind eye when they see someone else doing something unethical or dipping our own toes into the waters of unethical practices.

Mark said his career never recovered. His story is a reminder that there is never a positive side to succumbing to sin. He worried about losing not just his career but also his reputation in the community and his family. Through this experience, Mark recognized that his own conceit and arrogance were part of what led to his demise. He turned to God in repentance and now enjoys the peace that comes with accepting God's grace.

One unique aspect of Mark's story is how his guardian angel, Cate, guided him to the right path. God sends people into the lives of believers to serve as His messengers, whether they are living or have passed on. Another unique aspect of Mark's story is the strong symbolism wishing wells have in his life. Sometimes it can be helpful to have symbols of God's love and power in your life to remind you that He is the only life choice that will lead to eternal life.

Time for Personal Reflection

1. Have you ever done something at work that you knew was wrong, but you proceeded anyway? Find an affirmation or Bible verse you can commit to memory easily. Repeat it to yourself when you feel tempted. Don't allow yourself

to start sliding down that "slippery slope." Hebrews 2:18 says, "Because he himself suffered when he was tempted, he is able to help those who are being tempted." When you face temptation, remind yourself that Jesus faced it, too—and overcame it.

2. Have you ever wondered if someone who touched you deeply and provided divine guidance was in fact an angel? If so, you aren't alone. Don't be afraid to share that experience with others. You may be surprised to learn how many others (like Mark Faris and like me) have had just such an experience.

3. Do you have a symbol of God's love that you can go to, such as the wishing well in Mark's case, or a cross you can carry with you? If not, what symbol can you use to remind yourself that God's grace is with you at all times?

Faith on Trial

Skip Masback is the founder and director of the Yale Youth Ministry Institute at Yale Divinity School and the Associate Director of the Yale Center for Faith & Culture.

According to a 2016 article published in *The Atlantic*, employees of all ages are unhappy with their work. Jim Harter, Gallup's chief scientist for workplace management and well-being, weighed in, and his views were summed up in the article this way:

Those in midlife are slightly unhappier than those of other ages, and for different reasons. Harter says they are particularly likely to complain of feeling "locked into" their careers—stuck in neutral as their junior colleagues zip along. Although the mid-career slump cuts across industries and income levels, he notes that college-educated employees report greater unhappiness than do those who stopped at high school. He believes that highly educated people may have higher expectations, and may therefore find career disappointments more bitter.[6]

Employees who are unhappy in their jobs hurt productivity, and "Gallup has found that, compared with engaged employees, actively disengaged workers of all ages are far likelier to report stress and physical pain. They have higher cortisol levels and blood pressure, and they are nearly twice as likely to be diagnosed with depression or to call in sick."[7]

Skip Masback is one of those highly educated people who found that the career he had worked so hard to excel in no longer fulfilled him. Fourteen years into his highly successful career as a corporate and public-interest litigator, Skip had a "look in the mirror" experience that drained the meaning and purpose from his work. There didn't seem to be any prospect that the long years of exhausting work would lead to the life of fulfillment and meaning he had imagined. In the midst of the emotional suffering that followed, an encounter with Jesus brought Skip assurance and hope that led to a profound change of vocation. He left his law practice to study Scripture, to take night courses at Georgetown University, and then to enter Yale Divinity School to prepare for ordination. He became the youth minister and then senior minister of one of the largest churches in Connecticut for nineteen years, supervising youth ministries that grew to serve more than seven hundred children.

When he experienced a call to help other churches build transformative youth ministries in 2013, Skip resigned from his pastorate and joined Professor Miroslav Volf as the managing director of Volf's Yale Center for Faith and Culture at Yale Divinity School. Skip is the founder and director of the Yale Youth Ministry Institute. His passion is to train youth ministers and resource transformative youth ministries throughout the United States and beyond. Skip has twenty-five years of experience in parish ministry, church revitalization, and ministry to youth.

Here is his story.

———————

Lord knows my mom had tried. She cherished the Bible-centered formation she had received in her little Manchester, Georgia, Baptist church, and she was determined to find the same experience for her children. Never mind that she and my dad had moved from Georgia to New York—she just kept scouting churches until she found an American Baptist church founded by fellow Georgians who had moved north from Atlanta.

I loved that little church. It was a wonderful expression of what Atlantans used to call the "New South": conservative enough to emphasize "old school" biblical education but liberal enough to participate in the civil rights movement and welcome the Rev. Dr. Martin Luther King Jr. to its pulpit in 1958.

Sunday mornings were filled with Bible memorization games and prayer, Sunday afternoons and evenings were reserved for junior and senior high fellowship groups, and Wednesday nights saw us back in church for junior choir practice. I can still remember the raised sandbox of my nursery school room, the smell of the fellowship hall on Sunday morning, and the Southern accents of the moms and dads who taught my Sunday school classes.

Questioning the Message

But all the maternal determination in the world couldn't guarantee a seamless transmission of the faith. When my ninth-grade English teacher assigned readings in Edith Hamilton's *Mythology: Timeless Tales of Gods and Heroes*, an agnostic light bulb flickered on in my mind: Maybe myths are only placeholders to explain mysteries beyond the reach of reason? Maybe we believe in sun gods until we understand astronomy, crop gods until we understand agriculture, and war gods until we understand anthropology? Maybe we hold on to our Christian stories only because we haven't yet figured out our first origins and our ultimate destinations?

I didn't presume to know the answers to these ultimate questions, but I remember thinking that human reason was like a light of truth that was steadily advancing to illuminate all of reality. It seemed more "heroic" to stand courageously before the receding shadows of the unknown than to cling to the transient comfort of myths. After all, I wouldn't want to have been the last human to believe in a rain god, and I didn't want to be the last one to believe in a creator God.

Of course, none of this reduced my weekly round of church activities. My Southern mom wasn't much into asking my brothers and me if we wanted to go. We just went to church. That's what our family did. I may have squirmed some when the pastor turned to stories of virgin birth or resurrection, but I still loved the sense of communal fellowship, the space for ethical reflection, the care of the young adults who led our youth groups, and the weekly games of touch football in the church parking lot.

By the time I got to high school, my classmates and I were flowing with the currents of youthful idealism—currents that swelled into tidal forces when I entered college in 1969. We were engaging the heady ideas of an "Enlightenment" education in the classroom and pouring our energies into the twin causes of "peace and freedom" on weekends. Like many of my college classmates, I marched on Washington, protested in New Haven, worked on the student strike, "cleaned for Gene" McCarthy, and went door to door campaigning for George McGovern.

I don't think I went to church one time in four years of college … except when I was home on vacation. My mom still wasn't much into asking if I wanted to go to church. We just went.

Professional Exhaustion amidst Personal Plenty

My passion for social justice issues inspired a turn to law school and then the practice of law in a Washington, DC, firm with a national reputation for public-interest lawyering. Because I was now a husband and father, my maturing aspirations included being (1) a good husband, 2) a good father, 3) a servant of the public interest, and 4) an ethical lawyer.

Christian faith and identity weren't on my list, but I had married a woman of deep Christian faith. If I had been going to church while growing up to keep my mom happy, I was going to church now to keep my wonderful wife happy.

For fourteen long years, I poured my best energies into pursuing an elusive balance of family, work, and worthy causes. An annual round of all-nighters and long weekends working on cases yielded flourishing corporate and pro bono litigation practices that may have glittered to outsiders, but inside I was slowly hollowing out, worn down and contorted by the toll. When a crisis led to a proverbial "look in the mirror," I found myself dissolving in tears.

I recognized that if I were to die in my sleep, the epitaph wouldn't approach the goals I had set for myself. I had the most wonderful wife and family in the world, but you can hardly be a good husband or father when you are so often on the road taking testimony, sleeping on a cot at the office, staggering home after the kids have gone to sleep, and heading back to work before sunrise. One morning, my son had struggled out of bed at 6:30 and raced into our bedroom only to ask my wife, "Has Daddy gone home already?"

I could roll out a list of meaningful public-interest cases I had handled, but the ever-expanding load of commercial cases always pressed the pro bono work to the margins. And, while I never violated the letter of legal ethics, the intensity of our litigation often meant edging too close to the spirit of those boundaries.

Simply put, after seventeen years of exhausting effort, my life had become distorted; it no longer made sense. Moreover, as a name partner of a firm whose soaring income ran just a lap ahead of its soaring expenses, I didn't see any way off the hamster wheel. I couldn't slow down, I couldn't stop, and the relentless pace offered little prospect of living the life I had envisioned.

I don't know whether the right label for what I experienced next is "spiritual crisis" or some form of depression. All I know is that I couldn't stop crying. Well, I didn't actually cry while my wife and kids were awake. They were always a balm. But day after day, I found myself crying on the Washington Metro as I rode to work, and night after night, I found myself quietly crying myself to sleep.

At first, I presumed I could work my way through the crisis with the same tools and tenacity that had served me well with other challenges. I delegated more work to junior partners and associates. I hired a chauffeur so I could sleep on the way to and from work. I walked our three miles of bridle trails before work each morning. I even learned a secular meditation form, meditating on the number one. Nothing worked. I was buoyed by time I could spend with my warm, supportive wife and kids, but my cases still made it hard to get home. And I was still weeping all the way to work and all the way home.

A Life-Changing Event

One day, an evangelist working a Washington Metro station shoved a tract containing Bible excerpts into my hand, and I absent-mindedly folded it into my wallet. There it remained, wadded up and unread, for weeks. I doubted there was a God waiting to answer any prayer the Scriptures might inspire. And, even if there were a God, I figured that God would know my pleas were born out of desperation rather than faith.

Then again, I was desperate, and I had exhausted every other tool, technique, or trick I could think of to arrest my slide. One day, as my morning train wended its way downtown, I finally reached into my wallet and slipped the tract out. At first, the listless exercise of scanning excerpts seemed just as pointless as I had expected: "No, this verse seems meaningless ... No, this claim is incredible ... No, I don't even understand what this story means."

But eventually I came to the Nativity story in Luke's gospel—the story most churches enact in their Christmas pageants. And as I scanned the verses, I came to the account of the shepherds:

And there were in the same country shepherds abiding in the field, keeping watch over their flock by night. And, lo, the angel of the Lord came upon them, and the glory of the Lord shone round about them: and they were sore afraid. And the angel said unto them, Fear not: for, behold, I bring you good tidings of great joy, which shall be to all people. (Luke 2:8–10 KJV)

As I read the words "And the angel said unto them, Fear not," something happened. I wish I were a gifted enough writer to articulate for you that "something" with precise, fresh language. But I have never understood what happened with precision, and I don't have the talent to summon words that don't sound pretty much like every other heartfelt "testimony" I've rejected as incredible over the years.

All I know for sure is that there came a moment when I realized that I wasn't crying anymore. As the train clicked and clacked along the tracks, I was overtaken by a new sense of calm, a peace. I didn't jump up and cry, "Thanks be to God—I'm saved!" I just sat silently, savoring the immense relief of the absence of anguish.

Except, even as my shoulders relaxed into the relief of the moment, my mind kicked into litigation mode, scanning the evidence of what had just happened. Running a quick forensic checklist seemed to surface three broad possibilities. Had Yahweh, creator of everything that is, suddenly reached into a Washington Metro car to heal a suffering mind? It felt just like that. Or perhaps all I could say for sure is that I had been drawn into a transcendent encounter with a spiritual power beyond human description. Maybe my personal understanding of a biblical God was just a consequence of having been raised in a church. Or maybe my experience was a psychological phenomenon, a series of neurons firing at the intersection of my mental suffering on the one hand and all those Bible verses I had memorized as a kid on the other.

I realize this story might read better if it were simpler, if I could just testify to the healing power of God and close by giving thanks for His steadfast love. But that's not how I understood my experience.

The experience was simple: I was no longer crying. I was at peace. But the explanation, the source, of that experience was not simple. It was ambiguous, and my litigator's instincts told me that no amount of rehearsing the evidence was ever going to resolve the ambiguity. All I knew for sure was that something had happened. Something consequential. Something comforting. Something wonderful.

It was wonderful, but it proved to be passing. By the next day, I could feel myself slipping back toward the abyss. Reaching into my wallet, I pulled out the fraying tract and thumbed through to Luke's Nativity story. Sure enough, the angel's "Fear not" again restored peace to my soul.

Jesus on the Metro Train

For some days, my commutes were marked by the same pattern. Every time I felt myself slipping, I read my way through the angel's pronouncement of Good News to the shepherds. Every time I read the passage, I felt my soul restored. Of course, it's not a very long passage, so within a few days, I had committed the passage to memory. Now I found myself riding back and forth to work, eyes closed, steadily repeating the passage like a mantra to hold back the darkness.

One day, I opened my eyes in the midst of my recitations to see Jesus sitting calmly on the Metro seat facing mine. He looked pretty much the way He's pictured in popular paintings (minus the blue eyes and blond hair). He had long hair and a beard and was wearing the familiar simple robe and sandals. All I remember Him saying was some gentle words of assurance: "Skip, do not be anxious. I am going to take care of everything." As quickly as He had come, He was gone.

I sat for a long while resting in the peace His words had invoked. But soon enough, my mind was running its forensic trap line again. Had Jesus, the Son of the Most High, just appeared on the Washington Metro and "saved" me, just as promised by the faded signs on Southern tobacco barns? It felt just like that. Or maybe I had just recited my little Bible verse so many times that I had drifted into a daydream. Perhaps, but wouldn't that be like the visions recorded in

Scripture? Or maybe I had fallen asleep in mid-recitation, but again, wouldn't that be like the dreams experienced by the Josephs and Jacobs of Scripture?

The Mystery of Transformation

No amount of rehearsing the encounter resolved the mystery, and, again, my litigator's instincts told me that no amount of analysis was ever going to resolve the ambiguity. But this thought led to another: Maybe religious experiences are almost always inherently ambiguous. Maybe even the great epiphanies of Scripture were ambiguous when first experienced—before the process of telling and retelling the stories over centuries smoothed out the rough edges and filled in the ambiguities with certitude.

In fact, maybe every human community that has ever walked the ups and downs of life together has experienced variants of such encounters in ways that strengthened them in times of trial, lifted hope in times of despair, and added radiance to times of joy. Every community, that is, except for my little demographic fragment of skeptical yuppies who had decided we were too smart for it all and had managed to maroon ourselves in the wilderness, cut off from God.

I knew I couldn't explain what had happened, but neither could I let it rest. The encounter set me off on a furious faith quest to reconcile what my heart knew was one of the most important experiences of my life and what my head said was impossible or worse.

I didn't know where my faith quest would lead, but I knew that if my journey ever led to finding a way to make peace between my believer's heart and my skeptic's mind, then it would lead to a ministry. It probably wouldn't be a ministry to folks of orthodox or settled faith. They might not understand, and they almost certainly wouldn't be helped by the fruits of my struggles. More likely, it would be a ministry to folks puzzling over their own faith, or searching for their own answers, or wondering whether to trust the little ambiguous experiences they had had for themselves.

My journey since Jesus promised, "Skip, do not be anxious. I am going to take care of everything," has not always been easy. But Jesus has kept His promise through good times and bad for twenty-eight years and counting. Thanks be to God.

As a pastor, there are a lot of Bible verses Skip has turned to for strength and comfort; those shown below are just a few of his favorites. The first verses listed, Luke 2:8–10, are the ones he mentioned in his story in which the angel told the shepherd, "Fear not."

And there were in the same country shepherds abiding in the field, keeping watch over their flock by night. And, lo, the angel of the Lord came upon them, and the glory of the Lord shone round about them: and they were sore afraid. And the angel said unto them, Fear not: for behold, I bring you good tidings of great joy, which shall be to all people. (Luke 2:8–10 KJV)

The LORD is my shepherd; I shall not want. He maketh me to lie down in green pastures: he leadeth me beside the still waters. He restoreth my soul: he leadeth me in the paths of righteousness for his name's sake. Yea, though I walk through the valley of the shadow of death, I will fear no evil: for thou art with me; thy rod and thy staff, they comfort me. Thou preparest a table before me in the presence of mine enemies: thou anointest my head with oil; my cup runneth over. Surely goodness and mercy shall follow me all the days of my life: and I will dwell in the house of the LORD for ever. (Psalm 23:1–6 KJV)

God's Love in Christ Jesus

What, then, shall we say in response to these things? If God is for us, who can be against us? He who did not spare his own Son, but gave him up for us all—how will he not also, along with him, graciously give us all things? Who will bring any charge against those whom God has chosen? It is God who justifies. Who then is the one who condemns? No one. Christ Jesus who died—more than that, who was raised to life—is at the right hand of God and is also interceding for us. Who shall separate us from the love of Christ? Shall trouble or hardship or persecution or famine or nakedness or danger or sword? As it is written: "For your sake we face death all day long; we are considered as sheep to be slaughtered." No, in all these things we are more than conquerors through him who loved us. For I am convinced that neither death nor life, neither angels nor demons, neither the present nor the future, nor any powers, neither height nor depth, nor anything else in all creation, will be able to separate us from the love of God that is in Christ Jesus our Lord. (Romans 8:31–39)

The New Life in Christ

Therefore, I urge you, brothers and sisters, in view of God's mercy, to offer your bodies as a living sacrifice, holy and pleasing to God—this is your true and proper worship. Do not conform to the pattern of this world, but be transformed by the renewing of your mind. Then you will be able to test and approve what God's will is—his good, pleasing and perfect will. (Romans 12:1–2)

My Thoughts on Skip's Story

One of the aspects of Skip's story that I find interesting is how he tried so hard to intellectually explain his spiritual experience. A lot of people of faith do this; they try to find the logic in God's superhuman power, and they just can't do it. Skip said, "My litigator's instincts told me that no amount of analysis was ever going to resolve the ambiguity." This is the case with a lot of highly intelligent and educated people. There comes a point when they must simply accept God's omnipotence, omnipresence, and omniscience.

I think Skip's unique experience has an important place in our church community. While some people accept Jesus Christ as their savior as children and then lead long, happy lives as Christians, that isn't the case for everyone. Skip's story is a reminder that sometimes it takes a lot of questioning and reconciling before we accept Christ. But after going through that frustrating type of struggle with ourselves, it is a blessing when we finally surrender attempts at ironclad logic and reason and accept His perfect grace in our lives. Skip can lead people who have been through similar experiences to Christ in a way that others cannot.

Skip has developed a valuable ministry to people he describes as "folks puzzling over their own faith, or searching for their own answers, or wondering whether to trust the little ambiguous experiences they have had for themselves." I think his journey under God's grace is truly remarkable.

Time for Personal Reflection

1. Have you ever invested years of your life in a career or other endeavor that turned out to be unfulfilling? How long did you feel unfulfilled before you made a change? How did a change affect your personal growth, development, and state of mind?

2. If you have been saved, did you grapple with intellectually understanding the supernatural aspects of the experience, like Skip did? At what point did you finally accept it as God's divine transformation of your life? Or have you done so?

3. In what ways and to what extent do you think stories of experiences like Skip's can be used to the benefit of a faith community?

Healing Insights

- For many Americans, work is a huge part of their identities, and they spend a good portion of their lives trying to carve out successful careers. For that reason, having problems at work can be devastating in many ways—financially, emotionally, and in terms of relationships. It is important that people keep their work lives aligned with God's will, just as they do their personal lives.

- Rationalizing dishonest actions leads to a "slippery slope" that can damage reputation, family life, and livelihood. Integrity, or "doing what's right," will always pay off.

- Regardless of how successful you might become in your career, that career choice might not be what God had planned for you. In every professional endeavor, you should always pray for God's guidance and for His will to be done.

- If God calls you into a vocation that serves Him more directly, it is likely that He will make use of the skills, talents, and experiences through which He has already blessed you.

A Prayer for Those Struggling with Career-Related Challenges

The stories in this chapter are about crises related to two very different career-related challenges, including a top executive's serious ethical lapse that landed him in prison and an attorney's successful career that lost its luster. If you are facing any type of crisis in your career, here is a prayer that you can modify to reflect your situation:

Dear heavenly Father, thank you for the gifts of my education, skills, talents, and professional experiences. My career is both my livelihood and a large part of my identity here on earth.

Please help me sort out the difficulties I am having at work. If this is not the path You want for me, please gently nudge me in the right direction, and please give me the wisdom to see where You are leading me.

Father, I trust you completely. Please forgive me for those times when I have been stubborn and have insisted on trying to solve my job-related issues by myself, without Your divine guidance. I pray that You will heal the hurt that this situation has caused other people and me. Teach me to make choices that align with Your will for my life, dear God.

In Jesus' name I pray. Amen.

6

RISING ABOVE
FAMILY ISSUES

The bonds that tie families together are some of the strongest human connections there are. Seeing our loved ones suffer, whether they are grandparents, parents, siblings, or children, is agonizing.

Family dynamics can be complicated. For example, although people love their family members, members of the family may exhibit behaviors or personality traits that concern them. And it can be frustrating when love and concern for a family member isn't enough to free him or her from the clutches of an addiction, a bad relationship, or a lifestyle that can't be condoned.

The stories in this chapter demonstrate the helplessness, anxiety, disappointment, and/or shame families can feel when their children are facing life-changing or life-threatening situations. God's grace is remarkably powerful—enough to transform all those emotions into acceptance and comfort and to channel its recipients' responses into empowered future Christian service.

Surrendering to Faith:
What Seizures Taught Us

In the summer of 2016, Shane and Sandra Shepherd saw Jackson's neurological pediatrician, Dr. James Pappas, and took this photo of him with Jackson.

According to WebMD, "fever, a lack of oxygen, head trauma, or illness [can] bring on a seizure. People are diagnosed with epilepsy when they have seizures that occur more than once without such a specific cause. In most cases—about seven out of 10—the cause of the seizures can't be identified. This type of seizure is called 'idiopathic' or 'cryptogenic,' meaning that we don't know what causes them."[1]

Some physicians say that children rarely suffer long-term harm as a result of a seizure and that most seizures can be controlled with medication. Still, seizures are scary experiences for children and their parents.

⁂

I am on the board of directors for a company for which Shane Shepherd is the supervisor of the Corporate Security Department. One of his group's duties is to transport board members from their hotel to the office to attend meetings. Shane and I struck up a conversation in the hotel lobby, and he mentioned that he is a deacon and the security coordinator for his church. I told him about my first book, *God Revealed.* That led to an inspiring conversation about his son's miraculous healing and his own faith journey.

Shane and his wife, Sandra, faced an ordeal filled with anguish and uncertainty when their infant son began having seizures. The seizures continued for several years, taxing the family's strength, resources, and relationships. They learned how to pray boldly and ask God to relieve their son of the seizures. Here is their story.

———————————

My wife and I married in 1994. I was raised Catholic, and she was a Methodist. Neither of us had attended church since high school. She got pregnant with our first child in late 1998. We lost the baby in the first trimester. She got pregnant with our second child in the fall of 1999. We lost that baby in the first trimester too.

Late in 1999, my wife underwent some tests, but doctors could find no medical issues that could be causing the losses. In the spring of 2000, she got pregnant again, and we lost the baby in the beginning of the second trimester. We found out that it had been an ectopic pregnancy, with the fetus in the fallopian tube.

These losses, combined with my part-time career as a reserve police officer, caused our marriage to become very unstable.

Further testing revealed that the losses were a result of problems with my wife's fallopian tubes. That meant our only options for having children were adoption or in vitro fertilization (IVF). My wife didn't want to adopt, so, we began treatment for IVF retrieval and placement late in 2002. In January 2003, we were thrilled to find out that we were going to have twin boys. They were born via emergency C-section. It was extremely stressful for both of us.

Twins and Seizures

The boys weighed 4 pounds, 9 ounces and 2 pounds, 7 ounces. The smaller baby, Jackson, had 0 percent body fat at birth. He was born "not breathing." I believe the only reason they survived is because they arrived during shift change for the hospital staff. Had the boys not been born during shift change, there would not have been enough staff to give each of the boys the medical attention they required. As it was, we ended up having two NICU doctors and many nurses there to help save the boys' lives. Jackson spent three weeks in the Neonatal Intensive Care Unit, and our bigger baby, Ryan, spent two weeks there.

At the age of three, Jackson had a seizure. There was no trigger, no cause. He underwent tests in the hospital, and that produced no answers. The doctors kept us overnight for observation, but ultimately sent us home with him and with no answers.

My sister, who is a Christian and a member of Lebanon Christian Church (LCC), was there. She was with some other people, later identified as LCC members we didn't know. My sister said they were there to support us. There was someone from LCC in the waiting room for us during that entire twenty-four hours we were there, praying for us and the medical staff.

Three days later, Jackson had another seizure, and we took him back to the hospital. After more tests, we still had no answers. The doctor, who was not a pediatric neurologist, prescribed an anticonvulsant medication that we found out later, had not been approved by the FDA for children under the age of six. Again, my sister and others from LCC waited with us at the hospital.

Discouragement to Recovery

Jackson's seizures increased over time. He had three different types of seizure activity: tonic-clonic (which causes muscles to jerk), myoclonic (which causes brief, shock-like jerks of the muscles), and atonic (seizures that cause the muscles to go limp). For nearly a year, we went through medication changes and tests. Jackson was having more than 75 to 150 seizures a day. The quality of life for all of us was terrible, and eventually I felt like giving up. I was angry at God for finally giving us children, only to handicap one of them. I felt like God was mocking me. I felt like I was a joke, and this was the punch line. I felt as though God had put us through the losses to test us and that we had failed that test, so He gave us more trials to discourage us—and it was working. I decided that, in our desperation to reverse the negative thoughts, we needed to appeal to God through prayer to help us. So we began going to LCC, although we had no intention of becoming members.

In May 2006, we visited Jackson's neurologist. We began talking about Jackson's quality of life. He suggested that we think about getting Jackson a helmet to protect his head from the "drop" seizures. We had also begun discussing going to the Cleveland Clinic to have a neuro-interrupter implanted to help control Jackson's seizures. He also changed one of Jackson's medications as a last option. He said there was less than a 2 percent chance that these measures would result in gaining control of Jackson's seizure activity.

To our extreme joy, miraculously, in July, Jackson had his last major seizure. The meds were working! To us, this was clearly God's intervention that provided Jackson with exactly what was needed.

In December 2006, God's marvelous grace and gift of healing led us to be baptized and to become members of LCC.

Over the next four years, Jackson remained on medication. In 2010, we began weaning him from seven different medications. He hasn't had a seizure for ten years. The only way we got through this was through God's grace and love.

Sharing Our Knowledge

While Sandra and I were relishing the fact that Jackson's seizures had ceased, we knew he could relapse at any time, and we would be back to square one. However, we continued to attend seminars and find out everything we could about seizure disorders. We told our pediatric neurologist that we would be willing to talk with any parents who were in a "hopeless" cycle of seizure disorder with their child. We said we could provide hope where they could find none. We talked about how we were struggling in our faith and how when we submitted to God's plan, we found His grace. We also told the doctor that he could talk about Jackson's case and the severity of it to people who were experiencing seizure disorder in their lives.

The veterinarian we've used since we got our first pet called us out of the blue one day and was noticeably upset. She said her daughter had experienced a series of seizures similar to how they began to occur with Jackson. She was full of questions, and we (Sandra, mostly) talked to her and helped her get in touch with our pediatric neurologist. We explained to her what to expect, how to react, and what types of questions to ask the doctors. She is a medical professional, but she was asking us about this disorder.

She knew about Jackson's seizures because we had a diabetic cat that had seizures, and this veterinarian had treated the cat for years. She knew what we had been through with Jackson, so we were the ones she called to ask questions. I believe God orchestrated our paths crossing. Her daughter's seizure disorder is now controlled through medications, with little to no seizure activity. Every time the vet sees us, she thanks us for educating her about the condition and for putting her in touch with our pediatric neurologist.

Encouraging Bible Passages

During the extremely difficult years in which we dealt with Jackson's seizures, my wife and I read the story of the healing of a demon-possessed boy in Matthew:

> When they came to the crowd, a man approached Jesus and knelt before him. "Lord, have mercy on my son," he said. "He has seizures and is suffering greatly. He often falls into the fire or into the water. I brought him to your disciples, but they could not heal him." "You unbelieving and perverse generation," Jesus replied, "how long shall I stay with you? How long shall I put up with you? Bring the boy here to me." Jesus rebuked the demon, and it came out of the boy, and he was healed at that moment. Then the disciples came to Jesus in private and asked, "Why couldn't we drive it out?" He replied, "Because you have so little faith. Truly I tell you, if you have faith as small as a mustard seed, you can say to this mountain, 'Move from here to there,' and it will move. Nothing will be impossible for you.' " (Matthew 17:14–20)

Now, while we didn't think that Jackson was "demon-possessed," it certainly hit home that we needed a stronger faith that God would heal Jackson. That was the verse we would revisit when we were down and we knew we needed fervent prayer.

Also during that time, a family member quoted a Bible verse to me, and for the life of me, I couldn't remember where it was from for the longest time. It was a while later that I heard the same verse quoted in a Moody radio sermon. Here it is: "Let us not become weary in doing good, for at the proper time we will reap a harvest if we do not give up" (Galatians 6:9).

Prior to this miracle in our lives, my faith was not very strong. This verse would linger in the back of my mind sometimes to remind me to "keep the faith." I am, by self-admission, a control freak. When something is out of my control (that I haven't been trained to handle), I am, at best, difficult to deal with. I can handle the uncertainty of an intruder, an active shooter, or a medical emergency because I've been trained on how to deal with those uncertain situations. But when it comes to things clearly out of my control, in the past I had not relied on God.

Before this situation happened, "letting go and letting God" was not easy or natural for me. God is patient in teaching us to rely on, and trust in Him. It took the desperation of Jackson's situation and the faithfulness and prayers of our Christian friends for us to come to our senses and realize that in the future, in both good times and difficult times, we must put our faith in Him. We were most certainly empowered and guided by God's greatest gift—the gift of grace.

My Thoughts on Shane's Story

Sometimes it is difficult, even for believers, to trust God in a crisis situation because they think their own specialized training or knowledge should be sufficient. But it is not. I believe God allows crises to surface in people's lives to remind them that He is in control, so they don't need to be. That is such a relief, isn't it? You don't have to control, handle, and fix everything. As Shane discovered, you can place your faith in Him during both the good times and the bad.

Time for Personal Reflection

1. Do you have tendencies toward being a "control freak," which is how Shane described himself? If so, do you find it difficult to "let go and let God"? Sometimes it takes life's greatest trials to make us realize, as Shane says, that "in the future, in both good times and difficult times, we must put our faith in Him."

2. Shane says that "God's marvelous gift of healing" led his family to become baptized and to join their current church. Has there been a difficulty in your life that ended up bringing you closer to God? If so, how has that changed your view of the reason for life's hardships?

Hope in Action:
Drugs, Prison, and Ministry

This is Brandon Bailey's high school graduation photo. He was already starting to use marijuana.

There was a time when parents worried about their adolescent or young-adult children's use of marijuana and alcohol. Then cocaine became the drug of choice. Today, opioids have become the fastest-growing drug problem throughout the United States. The American Society of Addiction Medicine (ASAM) defines opioids as a class of drugs that includes the illicit drug heroin, as well as the licit, or legal, prescription pain relievers oxycodone, hydrocodone, codeine, morphine, fentanyl, and others.[2]

According to the ASAM, "drug overdose is the leading cause of accidental death in the United States, with 47,055 lethal drug overdoses occurring in 2014. Opioid addiction is driving this epidemic, with 18,893 overdose deaths related to prescription pain relievers and 10,574 overdose deaths related to heroin in 2014."[3]

After the White House announced a plan to allocate $5 million toward combating heroin use and trafficking in August 2015, *US News & World Report* published a revealing article that provided sobering statistics on America's skyrocketing drug problem. Between 2002 and 2013, the rate of heroin-related overdose deaths had increased 286 percent. Citing data from the Centers for Disease Control, the article noted that nine in ten people who were using heroin were using it with at least one other drug, and most were using it with at least three other drugs—illustrating how the heroin epidemic and the opioid epidemic were fueling each other in a vicious cycle. The article stated, "People are forty times more likely to be addicted to heroin if they are addicted to prescription painkillers. ... In fact, the number of overdose deaths from prescription pain medication is larger than those of heroin and cocaine combined."[4]

The authors of a 2012 study by the National Center on Addiction and Substance Abuse at Columbia University (CASA Columbia) reported that "40 million Americans age 12 and over meet the clinical criteria for addiction involving nicotine, alcohol, or other drugs. ... Meanwhile, another 80 million Americans fall into the category of risky substance users, defined as those who are not addicted, but use tobacco, alcohol and other drugs in ways that threaten public health and safety."[5] This statistic likely reflects primarily smokers who are habituated to nicotine.

Drug addiction destroys lives—not just through overdoses, but through the destruction of families and the cost to society in terms of health care expenditures, increased crime to support drug habits, and lost work productivity.

When children go astray, despite having a loving, structured upbringing, parents can experience myriad emotions. They can withdraw into shame or denial, which can make it difficult for them to face the situation and seek help. They can let the feelings of rejection, anger, pain, and sorrow lead them to lash out at their children and even disown them.

It takes great courage on parents' part to have a loving response when a child gets involved in illegal or illicit activities. It requires a delicate balance of setting boundaries while still loving the child. What you can and should do is place that child into the loving arms of Jesus through constant prayers of supplication: "Be joyful in hope, patient in affliction, faithful in prayer" (Romans 12:12).

From the story of the prodigal son in the Bible, it is clear that the appropriate response to a child's straying is love and forgiveness. This passage from Luke describes the wayward boy's homecoming. The father did not shun his son or lecture him about his poor choices. He welcomed him with open arms and celebrated his return:

> But while he was still a long way off, his father saw him and was filled with compassion for him; he ran to his son, threw his arms around him and kissed him. The son said to him, "Father, I have sinned against heaven and against you. I am no longer worthy to be called your son." But the father said to his servants, "Quick! Bring the best robe and put it on him. Put a ring on his finger and sandals on his feet. Bring the fattened calf and kill it. Let's have a feast and celebrate. For this son of mine was dead and is alive again; he was lost and is found." So they began to celebrate. (Luke 15:20–24)

Similarly, the following verse shows God's expectation for people of faith to love and support children who have strayed: "What do you think? If a man owns a hundred sheep, and one of them wanders away, will he not leave the ninety-nine on the hills and go to look for the one that wandered off?" (Matthew 18:12).

When we pray for our children, we need to remember that God is the One who has the power to heal them and bring them back to righteousness. He assures us that He can and will renew the spirits of the broken:

I will give you a new heart and put a new spirit in you; I will remove from you your heart of stone and give you a heart of flesh. And I will put my Spirit in you and move you to follow my decrees and be careful to keep my laws. Then you will live in the land I gave your ancestors; you will be my people, and I will be your God. I will save you from all your uncleanness. I will call for the grain and make it plentiful and will not bring famine upon you. (Ezekiel 36:26–29)

The next story is about Terri and Dan Bailey of New Castle, Pennsylvania, whose thirty-one-year-old son, Brandon, is serving time in prison on drug charges. For the past nine years, they have presented a talk called "Brandon's Story" at churches and other organizations to help parents recognize the signs of drug abuse. Their hope is that one day Brandon will make those presentations himself. In January 2016, Dan became a state-certified recovery specialist so he can effectively counsel people who are struggling with drug addiction.

Here is their story, from Dan's viewpoint. Terri and Dan were transformed by grace and empowered to serve the Lord by touching the lives of others who experience the all-too-common and proliferating problem among young people today—drug abuse.

Brandon will be in prison for two more years. This has been going on for a good ten years. He goes in for a while, comes back out, does okay for about three months, then boom—it happens again, and he is back in for more charges. It has been a roller coaster ride.

In high school, Brandon did very well. He was a straight-A student and was featured in *Who's Who in America* a couple of years in a row. And he won national awards in English and math. But within six months of that, he was addicted. It started out with marijuana. He was actually smoking it in the house and blowing it out the window. He thought we would not smell it. But it was a good time of the year, so when he blew it out the window, it came upstairs and right into our window.

We talked to Brandon about it; he was seventeen or eighteen at the time. By the time you find out about it, chances are, your son or daughter has been smoking it or using it for a while.

Brandon's Downward Spiral

In his first semester of college, Brandon did pretty well. Early in his second semester, we noticed that things were different. We didn't know if it was a problem with a girlfriend or what. We went through our own denial and thought, "Well, we've talked so many times about drugs; that's not what it is. It's got to be something different." And he's a reserved person. He doesn't talk a lot, so he doesn't express a lot of things. But when he began taking money and jewelry from us, we found out that he had a problem.

And it only got worse. He began using OxyContin, which was widely available in this town. We had a few doctors who were distributing prescriptions left and right to anybody who wanted them. These doctors ended up in prison. They put probably fifty thousand OxyContin pills per month on the streets of New Castle. People would be lined up in the parking lot at the entrance to these doctors' offices before they even opened. So that's where Brandon probably got started. OxyContin is expensive, so Brandon started to burglarize homes, including my dad's. That was pretty nasty. That was the beginning of the end. At the height of Brandon's addiction, he admitted to doing eight 80 mg pills of OxyContin a day. That's $640 worth in a day. None of us can afford that.

Next, he began using heroin, and that was pretty much the end. It ruins people's lives. We call it the devil drug. A lot of drug dealers from the area between Pittsburgh, Cleveland, and Detroit have come here. Our district attorney and police department have done a wonderful job of trying to clean up our town, but there is a heavy influx of drugs. And it's mostly heroin now because it's cheap—it costs just $5 to $8 a bag. Someone estimated that there are probably eight thousand heroin users in our town of about twenty-three thousand.

"Brandon's Story" for Others

One morning as I was praying about it, I heard the faint voice of Jesus say to me, "You have to do something." I had no idea how to put together a program, but I accepted what Jesus asked me to do. In my profession, I was a training supervisor, teacher, and course developer. I know how to use PowerPoint to create presentations, so there was the vehicle. But I wanted to add video to it but didn't know how, so it took me about five or six months to teach myself how to add video. And that's how "Brandon's Story" was born. During the whole experience, God kept drawing us closer and closer to Him. This is an example of how Jesus turned something terrible from our standpoint into an opportunity to bring us to Him.

The presentation is a combination of our experiences as parents and the mistakes we made, but it also includes signs and symptoms of different types of drug use. The signs of marijuana use are going to be different from those of OxyContin and cocaine. So our advice to people is first to pay very close attention to your young ones. We go over the behavior signs, the changes in the circle of friends, and other changes in behavior to look for. We advise parents that if you notice these signs, ask your loved one about it. You will probably be met with denial, but we encourage them to get their young ones to professional counselors if they suspect something.

In this part of the country now, they are starting to drug-test athletes to make sure they are clean and not playing athletics under the influence of anything. But it doesn't catch everybody. Once people are addicted, they accelerate the drug use quickly. We suggest that parents tell their sons or daughters, "If you're clean and you're not using anything, then you won't have any issues with taking a drug test." You can buy drug tests. If they refuse to do the test, that raises a red flag.

Terri and I got a lot closer to Jesus through this experience. As we received God's grace during our ordeal, we realized that our strength was by the grace of God. It was this closeness to the Lord, and seeking His will for us, that led to our passion for helping other families facing this type of tragedy. This also led us to be "born again" into Christ as our sole source of salvation. Although we are sinners, we have developed a closeness with our Lord that does not quench a thirst for Him but actually intensifies our love for Him and our desire to do His will. We believe that by serving others in His name, He has let us know that we are on the right path.

About twenty-five years ago, Terri and Dan's pastor, Randy Crum, started the nonprofit Vision Ministries of Lawrence County to bring Jesus Christ into his city. From that ministry, Pastor Crum developed the Pathway to Freedom program in 2000 to bring Jesus Christ to people in addiction and recovery. Here are some comments from Pastor Crum about Brandon's recovery and about the program.

I think Brandon has a great shot at turning his life around because his parents know Christ. They have always prayed for him, and prayer moves the hand of God. I, of course, pray for Brandon too. I would say his state of mind is like everybody's state of mind in that particular age bracket. I have sons who are twenty-eight and thirty-three, and the world is constantly putting ideas into their heads, drawing them away from God. That's what the devil's plan is. He wants to draw people away, and I think he's using drugs to do that. In the end times, I believe that's what Satan will do to draw people away from good decisions. But we have to put these situations in the Lord's hands. You have to trust that the Lord is going to answer your prayer. It is God's battle, and God hears the prayers of His people.

I am an ordained minister, and I pastor a church, but I knew that my calling was more evangelistic. So I do crusades in schools, cathedrals, and other places. Five years ago, I designed a twelve-step program, like Alcoholics Anonymous, but God is the key—not *a* God, but *the* God—Jesus Christ. We use the program in our work with people who have addictions. There are a lot of addictions. The program is growing; about forty-five people attended our most recent meeting.

Recently we met with about ten people who are in various stages of recovery. While we were talking about Pathway to Freedom, I asked them, "Why are you able to sustain your long-term recovery when there are all kinds of triggers out there?" Their unanimous answer was "Jesus Christ." There is only one true pathway to freedom, and that is Jesus Christ.

Through Pathway to Freedom, we are working with the district attorney, the press, and the local judge to try to network that so that we can have some boots on the ground and get people the help they need. Dan developed a program of teaching, and I'm bringing the spiritual aspect into it—spirituality in recovery of addiction. The program is actually nondenominational because I'm a nondenominational pastor. That means I stand on the Word of God.

We can go where a lot of people can't go. If you are connected with the government, for example, they put restrictions on you. We are not restricted in that way. We're very bold about where we go, such as into the jails to talk to inmates. In fact, a few of the people who are now serving with us are people I witnessed to in the jails. They come out of jail and want to be the leaders of these efforts once they're clean. Who better to lead other people out of the darkness and into the light but the people who have made it out of the darkness and into the light?

The following are favorite Bible verses that give Dan and Terri inspiration and keep them going when times get tough:

Come to me, all you who are weary and burdened, and I will give you rest. (Matthew 11:28)

Jesus replied, "Very truly I tell you, no one can see the kingdom of God unless they are born again." (John 3:3)

Put on the full armor of God, so that you can take your stand against the devil's schemes. For our struggle is not against flesh and blood, but against the rulers, against the authorities, against the powers of this dark world and against the spiritual forces of evil in the heavenly realms. Therefore put on the full armor of God, so that when the day of evil comes, you may be able to stand your ground, and after you have done everything, to stand. (Ephesians 6:11–13)

My Thoughts on Dan's Story

Dan's story about his son, Brandon, reminds parents that they have to be on constant watch to ensure their children's safety. Brandon was an A student and had won awards in high school, yet it didn't take long for drugs to take over his life, and now he is serving a prison sentence. In 1 Peter 5:8 is this admonition: "Be alert and of sober mind. Your enemy the devil prowls around like a roaring lion looking for someone to devour." The faithful should trust God not just in times of obvious crisis but in every moment of every day, when hidden crises may be beyond their current awareness.

Time for Personal Reflection

1. Have you ever had a child's behavior spiral out of control, despite your best efforts to correct the situation? If so, what did you learn from the experience? At what point, if at all, did you turn to the Lord in prayer to ask for His intervention and guidance?

2. Have you forgiven yourself the way the Lord has forgiven you for any mistakes you believe you made in parenting?

3. If you have ever had a rebellious child, to what extent did you seek support from others, such as friends, church members, your pastor, or others? Were you embarrassed to let people know what was happening? Looking back, what would you do differently? If you are currently suspicious of a child's behavior and suspect potential drug use, step up your prayer life, and at the same time, seek professional assistance in confronting the situation.

Comfort beyond Measure

Jane Daly.

Caring for a family member can take its toll on a person's emotional, physical, and financial health. According to the Pew Research Center, at the end of 2012, "nearly half (47%) of adults in their 40s and 50s had a parent age 65 or older and were either raising a young child or financially supporting a child (age 18 or older). And about one in seven (15% percent) middle-aged adults was providing financial support to both an aging parent and a child."[6]

The stress associated with caring for two generations of family members can be overwhelming, especially if a caregiver has not planned for the additional expenditures of time, money, and effort. The term "caregiver burnout" is becoming more common today as more people take care of family members, often putting their own needs last.

Burnout can occur when caregivers don't get the help they need, or if they try to do more than they are able, either physically or financially. Caregivers who are "burned out" may experience fatigue, stress, anxiety, and depression. Many caregivers also feel guilty if they spend time on themselves rather than on their ill or elderly loved ones. It is

---

GRACE REVEALED

important to take the time necessary to care for yourself if you are a caregiver to others.

According to WebMD, caregiver burnout can result because caregivers often experience role confusion—in other words, they find it difficult to separate their role as a caregiver from their role as a child, spouse, or parent. Caregivers also can place unrealistic expectations and unreasonable burdens on themselves and become frustrated at their lack of control over a loved one's illness.[7]

If you are a caregiver, don't be reluctant to ask for help when you need it. The next story is about a remarkable woman who did not suffer caregiver burnout. Rather, she was humbled by the experience of caring for her father and her adult son simultaneously.

⸺⸺

Jane Daly's son and father experienced serious health issues simultaneously. Her son was diagnosed with inoperable cancer when he was only twenty-nine years old. And her father's failing health made it necessary for him to move to a care center, which he did not want to do. Jane spent the better part of 2009 flying back and forth to be with her son while dealing with the weekly emergencies associated with her father's declining health.

Jane is the author of two books: *Because of God's Grace: A Mother's Journey from Grief to Hope* and *The Caregiving Season: Finding Grace to Care for Your Aging Parent*.

I was my dad's favorite. I don't think my brothers will argue with me. He was hard on them, easy on me.

"That's my girl" is a phrase I heard often. He wasn't given to expressing his affection. I never remember him saying, "I love you." But *that's my girl* was the same thing.

My father's health began to decline a couple of years before his passing. He was diagnosed with polymyalgia, a nerve condition that

172

caused pain and tingling in his legs. Soon he needed a walker, and eventually he progressed to a wheelchair.

My husband, Mike, and I, along with my mom, convinced him to stop driving. This conversation is not for the faint of heart. Imagine you're the darling of your father's love, the apple of his eye, and in his eyes, you can do no wrong.

Then try saying, "Dad, we're taking your car keys." The fall from grace is a long way down, and the impact hurts.

My mom had stopped driving the previous year due to increasing macular degeneration. Mike and I did our best to make things easy for my parents in their new carless existence. I took Dad to his monthly swap meet so he could hang out with his buddies. Mike and I took turns driving Mom on errands and to the grocery store.

Still, Dad's health continued to worsen.

Life's Storms and God's Grace

As we note the gradual day-to-day changes in those we love, the "big picture" transformations often elude us. Then in one moment, we may suddenly witness a decade or two pass before our eyes. Our daughter seems to be an infant one day, and the next she's dressing up for prom or walking down the aisle to meet her groom. The same thing happens with our parents, except in reverse. We forever see them as youthful, vibrant people, playing baseball with us in the backyard, challenging us to a game of Scrabble, or handing out wisdom around the dinner table. They're growing older, but in our mind's eye, they stay the same.

That's one reason it's difficult to face the reality that our parents need our care. One minute they're chasing after our wobbly attempts to ride a two-wheeler, and the next we're helping them into the shower.

Life progresses, but not in a linear fashion.

It's a zigzag of messy moments, and sometimes it seems as if life's downpours lead to monsoons.

While I was dealing with the increasing number of Dad's falls, emergency room visits, doctors' appointments, and lab tests, our son called with devastating news.

"Mom, Dad, I have cancer. Again." He'd been in remission since his eighteenth birthday. He was now twenty-nine. He lived twelve hundred miles away.

I was like Sir Edmund Hillary, the first person to reach the peak of Mt. Everest. I was climbing up a treacherous mountain, exposed to the elements, battered by the wind, exhausted.

I needed God's grace.

D. L. Moody once said, "A man can no more take in a supply of grace for the future than he can eat enough for the next six months, or take sufficient air into his lungs at one time to sustain life for a week. We must draw upon God's boundless store of grace from day to day, as we need it." I love that quote. The more grace I needed, the more God supplied.

God knew I needed to spend time with my son. Although it didn't seem like His grace, I was laid off around the time he was diagnosed. My new job wasn't as demanding, and I was given the freedom to take off as much time as I needed. We crammed as much living as we could into the next several months.

The Most Difficult Thing I'd Ever Had to Do

There came a time during those fourteen months when our care for Dad wasn't enough. When an elder-care caseworker came to talk to us, we were armed with facts about why my father needed to make the move to a care facility. But the facts couldn't shield my heart from having to tell Dad he couldn't live at home anymore. He would no longer be able to wake up every morning next to my mom, his wife of more than sixty years. He couldn't prepare the coffee for breakfast the night before. There would be no more helping Mom by setting the table or emptying the dishwasher. His world would shrink to a seven-by-ten-foot bedroom.

As difficult as it was telling Dad he couldn't drive, this was worse. We let the elder-care advocate take the lead.

"Roger, I'm concerned about your safety and your overall health." Dad nodded. I don't think he knew where this was headed.

"Charleen can't keep calling 911 when you fall. You know she's not strong enough to pick you up, right?"

Dad murmured agreement.

"You have a couple of options I'd like to talk about."

She first suggested that he could have someone move in to offer around-the-clock care. Dad looked at Mom and asked, "How do you feel about that?"

Mom shook her head. "I'm not comfortable with it. I don't want a stranger in our house."

"Your second option is to move to a place where you'll have more hands-on care."

Dad visibly recoiled. "If I have to go into a convalescent hospital, I'll stop taking my meds and *die*." After one particularly nasty fall, he'd been hospitalized and then released to a convalescent hospital. He hated it.

The advocate nodded with understanding. "I know, but that's not what I'm talking about. Are you familiar with a board-and-care home?"

She explained he'd be in a home environment with his own room. A full-time caretaker would fix meals, help with bathing, and assist with any mobility issues.

I squirmed in my chair as she moved the conversation from "if" to "when." Guilt and grief in equal measure washed over me. Dad would likely die in that other place, away from his family, away from his darling daughter, his "chickie." I couldn't breathe. As I stepped outside to try to regain equilibrium, my cell phone rang. It was my daughter, Heather, calling to see how the conversation was going.

"This is the most difficult thing I've ever had to do," I told her. "More difficult than dealing with your brother's cancer. How can we make your grandpa move somewhere else?" It was like putting a child up for adoption. Or shoving my dad onto the streets. How could I force him to live with *strangers*?

Dad seemed resigned to the move. Mom cried, already grieving the separation. I was still focused on myself and my angst over having the dreaded conversation with Dad. I had little empathy for my mom.

Besides, my son needed me. This would allow me more flexibility to leave town, knowing Dad was in good hands.

God's Grace amid Heartbreak

What does God's grace look like when your son's diagnosis is terminal, and your father isn't expected to live more than a few months longer?

It's beautiful. Andrew Murray said it best in his book, *Abide in Christ*: "In Christ the heart of the Father is revealed, and higher comfort there cannot be than to rest in the Father's bosom. In Him the fullness of the divine love is revealed, combined with the tenderness of a mother's compassion—and what can comfort like this? In Him you see a thousand times more given you than you have lost."[8]

I'd heard countless times that God becomes more real to us during suffering. I found it to be true. The more I ran to Jesus, the more grace He poured out. He prepared my heart for my dad's passing. Six weeks later, Mike and I sat with our son when he took his last breath.

It hasn't been easy. I've walked through the valley of the shadow of death. It wasn't a brisk walk through the valley, and it wasn't a stroll in the forest. There was a treacherous precipice on one side, and an enemy waiting for my foot to slip off the edge. A rocky slide on the other side peppered me with loose pebbles, trying to keep me off balance.

In Psalm 23, the beautiful imagery of Jesus as the Good Shepherd comforted me during the agonizing fourteen-month period of Bobby's chemo and Dad's decline: "Even though I walk through the darkest valley, I will fear no evil, for you are with me; your rod and your staff, they comfort me" (Psalm 23:4).

All the way through my long walk through the valley, God's grace kept me from falling. With His rod on one side and His staff on the other, He guided my steps and kept me from stumbling.

Mother Care

Now I've begun a new journey: caring for my aging mother. The grace I've experienced helps me as I daily pour myself out for my mother's needs. I'm learning to look with more compassion on those in their twilight years, and with humility when I see other caregivers who do much more than I do.

Jesus told the disciples: "Remain in me, as I also remain in you. No branch can bear fruit by itself; it must remain in the vine. Neither can you bear fruit unless you remain in me. I am the vine; you are the branches. If you remain in me and I in you, you will bear much fruit; apart from me you can do nothing" (John 15:4–5). Through my suffering, I learned the truth of these two verses from the book of John. The more I abide in Him, the more grace He is able to pour out for my comfort.

I've been asked to speak to weary souls burdened by the weight of responsibility. I talk with people one-on-one, and I also speak to civic groups like the Rotary Club. I've applied to teach the subject at an upcoming pastors' and leaders' conference, and I'm working on a curriculum for an adult education course. I also share with people, mostly in one-on-one situations, my journey of hope and of God's unending grace. I walk them through Psalm 23.

God's grace is amazing.

My Thoughts on Jane's Story

It is by God's grace that Jane was able to understand how God worked in her life after losing her father and her son within six weeks of one another. Many people struggle to understand why God would let people suffer such a devastating loss. Jane acknowledges that "God becomes more real to us during our suffering." And now she is caring for her aging mother, with greater empathy for what people go through in their twilight years. Jane's experience is instructive for others looking for God's comfort—and His purpose—during their suffering.

Time for Personal Reflection

1. Jane says, "God becomes more real to us during suffering." To what extent do you agree with that? Looking back at your own life, do you find that you drew closer to God during the most difficult times? If so, does that enable you to appreciate those trials, even though they were painful?

2. In her story, Jane included this quote from author Andrew Murray: "In Him you see a thousand times more given you than you have lost." During times of loss in your life, to what extent have you been able to see how much God has given you, despite the great loss you endured? If you are not there yet, pray about it. Ask God to enable you to see the priceless gift of His grace in your life.

A Renewed Purpose— as an Octogenarian

John Claassen is shown with his first great-grandchild, Norah.

When parents enter their golden years, adult children worry about them. It can be painful to see them struggling to manage what used to be routine tasks. Aging can be a difficult process for the parents too. They often fear losing control of their ability to remain independent, and it is easy for them to quit enjoying life when their beloved spouse dies. One researcher on the topic of spousal loss says, "For those people dealing with the loss of a spouse, overcoming loneliness represents the greatest challenge in moving on with life afterward." He adds that health care professionals often diagnose bereaved spouses with depression when they are actually suffering from loneliness and grief.[9]

It is not uncommon for elderly couples to die within weeks, days, or even hours of one another. In an often-quoted 2008 study, researchers studied the "widowhood effect." They found that within the three months after one spouse dies, the chance that the other will follow is anywhere from 30 to 90 percent.[10]

The next story is about a man in his eighties who did just the opposite—he began a vibrant new life after his wife died.

Sue Craik is the director of Christian education at First United Methodist Church in Northville, Michigan. Her father, John Claassen, is eighty-nine years old. Sixty-four years ago, he had a near-death experience but emerged from it strong, healthy, and optimistic. He believes the Holy Spirit saved him because God had a purpose for his life. That turned out to be true; most of John's work in giving back to his community happened after he turned eighty-five years old. This is the first time John has ever written about his near-death experience.

John is a vibrant member of his retirement community, a volunteer who tutors children, and a joy and inspiration to everyone who knows him. After his wife died, instead of shutting himself off from people and giving up, as people sometimes do when they lose their spouse, John entered the most fulfilling stage of his life. After receiving God's unmerited grace, John is extending that grace to many others.

Here is John's story, first from his perspective and then from that of his daughter, Sue.

God has always been with me. Sometimes I didn't know it, but God has always been there.

I grew up in a religious family environment (Mennonite on both sides). In 1945–1946, as part of the US Army, I trained for the invasion of Japan, but World War II ended. Others died, and I feel close to them. I got to live the seventy-plus additional years they didn't get.

The Day I Almost Drowned

In the summer of 1951, I felt the urge to take some swimming lessons at the municipal pool in Visalia, California. I was twenty-four years old and had been working as a junior planning technician with the Tulare County Planning Commission for a year. The previous year, I had graduated from Iowa State College with a BS degree in landscape architecture on the GI Bill. I had taken swimming lessons as a kid, but I wasn't proficient enough and wanted to improve. The local Red Cross was offering lessons for adults, and I saw that as an opportunity.

There were several other young men in our learning group, so I felt quite at home. We liked our instructor, who sensed that the main reason we were there was to overcome our innate fear of water. He was right—a lot of our exercises took place in the end of the pool, where the water was fourteen feet deep. He had us jump in and sink to the bottom before surfacing, then tread water and swim to the side. We learned how to dog paddle and swim the sidestroke. These were good things to know, but the most important thing, I realized later, was that I felt comfortable in the water for the first time.

A year later, in the spring of 1952, my first wife, Carol, and I, along with a group of friends, decided to drive up into the Sierra Nevada Mountains to enjoy a Sunday-morning picnic along the Kaweah River. The river was placid most of the time, but this was in the spring, and the ample snow pack from the winter was melting in the mountains. The stream flow was heavy and rapid.

We had finished our picnic and were cleaning up and preparing to drive back to our various homes. Merrill Bird, an engineer and manager of a concrete pipe manufacturing company in Porterville, and I decided to play catch until it was time to leave. Merrill tossed the ball over my head, and it rolled into the water. I reached down to retrieve the ball and slid on a long, slippery rock into the river. In an instant, I was carried out into the center of the rushing water. I was wearing fatigues and combat boots—hardly the appropriate attire for the situation in which I found myself.

The water training I had received the previous summer kicked in. I guess you could call it "muscle memory." I started treading water; the current was too swift to swim in. Merrill never took his eyes off me. He knew I was in trouble. The others in our party laughed at my plight at first ... but quickly they, too, realized I was in grave danger. Many people had drowned in this white-water river.

I remember treading water as I was swept downstream. Merrill ran along the bank, following me. I was in the center of the river, where it was the deepest. I went under but quickly surfaced, only to go underwater a second time. Surprisingly, I didn't panic. Just the opposite—I stayed calm. The water was a beautiful aquamarine color with a bright light filtering through it. I remember envisioning an article in the Visalia newspaper with a headline stating, "Man Drowns in the Kaweah River." The next thing I remember was that I popped up to the surface again, and I felt firm footing under my feet. Merrill shouted to me, "Stay where you are! Don't move! I'm coming to get you!" He was my guardian angel. He waded in and brought me back to the shore. The others wrapped Merrill and me in towels. Then we got in our cars and drove home.

I was exhausted, both mentally and physically. I went to bed and slept until evening.

This event, which happened sixty-four years ago, has had a profound effect on my life. Was it a near-death experience (NDE)? Yes, I think so ... it bears many of the characteristics of an NDE. Did the Holy Spirit intervene because there were other plans for my life? The older I get (I'll be ninety this year), the more I believe this to be true. I believe God had a plan for me, and through God's grace, my life was extended to share this grace with others.

Although I have told my children this story before, this is the first time I have written about this experience. I think my children, and their children, should know this story. It just might save one of their lives one day.

Life after Divorce

Carol and I got divorced in 1953, and I made the life-changing decision to return to Nebraska, where I grew up.

From 1954 to 1984, I owned and ran a business in farm real estate. I enjoyed the work and liked owning my own business, though it presented many challenges throughout my career. After thirty years, I had learned much about not only business but also human nature. It wasn't always easy, but it certainly had its rewards.

I married Mary in 1957, and we had five children—three girls and two boys. In 1992, Mary, our youngest son, Aaron, and I moved from Nebraska to Oregon. Mary worked as a speech therapist, first for a private company, next for a county education system, and finally for an HMO. (The last one she thoroughly enjoyed … the first two, not so much.) Mary went through a severe depression in 1993. I was the caregiver for our quadriplegic son, Aaron, who has cerebral palsy. He was twenty-six at the time—the same age I was when I almost drowned. With the guidance of the Holy Spirit, the three of us worked through the trauma imposed on our family during a very trying period of about six months.

I unretired for about four years, from 1993 to 1997, and worked again as a rural appraiser for a man who had an established practice in Forest Grove near where we lived in Hillsboro. This was an enjoyable and educational experience. At the end of that period, Aaron moved away from home into an independent living apartment in Hillsboro. He is now forty-eight years old and still lives there.

In 2008, Mary was diagnosed with ovarian cancer.

The Day Mary Died

Mary chose the day she would die. In a startling and determined declaration in the deep, yet clarifying, hours of the night, she vocalized loud and clear, as if the realization were apparent and demanded proclaiming, "I want to die! I want to die!" She declared these words as if she were waking from a dream, yet the reality of it all was not to be denied. It was hard for me to hear those words. But we talked through the night, crying, planning, and making the decisions that had to be made ... together. Her life with the cancer had been going on for two years. During that time, her living with and managing the disease allowed her to be a part of three weddings—the marriage of our son, John, and two granddaughters—plus a family reunion. We traveled. Our life together was meaningful and valued. But she always knew there would be a time when this life would not be what she wanted, as the illness would take over, and her body would betray her to the point where the quality of her life would be unacceptable to her. We talked about her wishes at length.

On November 18, 2011, Mary died of ovarian cancer after two and a half years of treatment. When she died, there was no need for medical assistance, only palliative care until she chose the timing of her last breath. A weeks-long or even months-long hospice was not her plan. Once she had heard every child's voice and was confident in the timing that was crafted over a lifetime, Mary slipped away to the other side. I do believe she waits for me now. She is not counting the time or biding the time ... but confident of our reunion. As am I.

It's odd how after death occurs, life still moves boldly on. The simple act of driving home, as tedious and banal an act as it is, was required of me. My navigator no longer beside me, I journeyed the now well-worn road from hospital to home. But the car ride was not without technical trouble. Warning lights flashed, and I found myself pulling into a service station so that I could have the car checked. First things first. After resolving the car issue and turning my thoughts once again to the day at hand and all the strange and painful emotions it was sure to bring, I completed the paperwork with the service technician, only to notice the name tag on his work shirt ... Jesus. My Hispanic car savior was now my savior. Mary's presence was palpable. I felt her reaching out to me through "Jesus," and the message was clear to me: "Everything is going to be okay." It was God's grace, clear and true, at a pivotal moment in my life.

We are all connected ... and the glue that holds us together is love.

Life after Mary

Mary and I were married for fifty-four and a half years. After her death, I moved from Oregon to an independent-living apartment in Plymouth, Michigan. After more than two years of residency in my new home, I have found that the Holy Spirit has further plans for me. The joy and gratitude I feel for God's loving grace in my life have empowered and guided me, even at my advanced age, to give back by singing with the Village Choir (some solo work in a thirty-voice choir), promoting a reading program for our residents to help kids in Detroit's inner city (the residents and kids hit it off well), and now working on a strength-building program for nonagenarians. We need something like this to improve balance, endurance, and general fitness, primarily to guard against falls. This is not just for others; I will be ninety in two months and have a vested interest in such a program. While plans are in the works for a program at the residence, I have begun training at the gym myself so I can speak intelligently to the positive effects this strength training has on my life emotionally and socially, as well as physically.

Reflections of John's Daughter

This is new for my dad, all of this stepping out of his comfort zone ... the confidence, the inspiration he has acted on. He has always been an incredibly wonderful man, but this chapter in his life is truly something new and beautiful to behold.

Since my mother's death, my dad's invigorated connection to and encouragement from the Holy Spirit has led him to not only have the courage to leave his home of twenty-plus years but to embrace a life with purpose. He is recognized as a leader in his retirement community. He talks to everyone and offers a listening ear when others might walk on by. He has told me that he feels like he's going to church every time he walks out his front door. He stays attuned to where God might use him each day. He encourages folks to "tell their stories" and challenges them to embrace life.

When he had the inspiration to begin a reading program for children in inner-city Detroit, my dad totaled up the number of years of life represented by the more than two hundred residents at Independence Village—which came to more than seventeen thousand years—and pitched to the front office that this was how much knowledge and experience they had to offer. The administration made inquiries, and about a dozen residents have been taking the shuttle into Detroit to the Sarah Fisher Center and have been reading and connecting with high-risk children. He pitched it. Sold it. Inspired it. And his peers followed.

He talks with folks who visit his place, encouraging them in their decision to move into a retirement community ... not to market the facility but to help them through the process of change—both seniors and their children. The sales agents show his apartment regularly for that reason. He also sings in the choir and encourages others to get involved.

The strength-training program blows me away. How many ninety-year-olds do you know who decide to start dead-lifting weights at this stage of the game? When I tell my friends about his latest endeavor, I end with, "You know, I could not make this stuff up!"

My dad is beyond grateful for this next chapter in his life. He considers it all a bonus from God, and he's not about to squander it.

Dad has not belonged to a church since the early 1980s, so his spirituality for the past few decades has been very organic ... led by the Holy Spirit, he would say. But he tells me that he would not be the spiritual person with the attitude he has at ninety years old if my mom were still here. He has been given this long life to become the man he is today. Though he and my mom were a perfect fit—a great team in many ways—now is the best time of his life, spiritually. There is clarity in his understanding of God and the Holy Spirit that inspires me in ways that no Bible study can teach, preacher can preach, or hymn can convey. It is amazing to experience, and I thank God for it every day.

The following Bible verses are among John's favorites:

Why do you look at the speck of sawdust in your brother's eye and pay no attention to the plank in your own eye? How can you say to your brother, "Let me take the speck out of your eye," when all the time there is a plank in your own eye? You hypocrite, first take the plank out of your own eye, and then you will see clearly to remove the speck from your brother's eye. (Matthew 7:3–5)

Why do you call me, "Lord, Lord," and do not do what I say? As for everyone who comes to me and hears my words and puts them into practice, I will show you what they are like. They are like a man building a house, who dug down deep and laid the foundation on rock. When a flood came, the torrent struck that house but could not shake it, because it was well built. But the one who hears my words and does not put them into practice is like a man who built a house on the ground without a foundation. The moment the torrent struck that house, it collapsed and its destruction was complete. (Luke 6:46–49)

Ask and it will be given to you; seek and you will find; knock and the door will be opened to you. For everyone who asks receives; the one who seeks finds; and to the one who knocks, the door will be opened. (Matthew 7:7–8)

And he told them this parable: "The ground of a certain rich man yielded an abundant harvest. He thought to himself, 'What shall I do? I have no place to store my crops.' Then he said, 'This is what I'll do. I will tear down my barns and build bigger ones, and there I will store my surplus grain. And I'll say to myself, "You have plenty of grain laid up for many years. Take life easy; eat, drink and be merry." ' But God said to him, 'You fool! This very night your life will be demanded from you. Then who will get what you have pre-pared for yourself?' This is how it will be with whoever stores up things for themselves but is not rich toward God." (Luke 12:16–21)

John says he is "a big fan of the Holy Spirit," and he thinks this verse captures the essence of the Holy Spirit: "I pray that out of his glorious riches he may strengthen you with power through his Spirit in your inner being" (Ephesians 3:16).

My Thoughts on John's Story

I experienced such hope and joy reading John's story. It can be easy to think that aging and the death of a beloved spouse spell the end for the surviving spouse. But John is living proof that the survivor can become even more vibrant, active, and useful as he or she ages. Instead of lamenting what surviving spouses have lost, they need to find their next big adventure and declare, "The best is yet to come!"

Isaiah 46:4 says, "Even to your old age and gray hairs I am he, I am he who will sustain you. I have made you and I will carry you; I will sustain you and I will rescue you." God rescued John after Mary died. He brought him a renewed sense of purpose and satisfaction. And He can do the same for you.

Time for Personal Reflection

1. To what extent do you believe "the best is yet to come," even for people in their eighties? Do you know people who believe and demonstrate that, despite their advanced age? What can you learn from their positive outlook?

2. What do you want to accomplish in your seventies, eighties, and beyond that you would have never dreamed of until you read John's story? Think about it now. Take joy in planning your future and in ultimately making it a reality.

Healing Insights

- Substance abuse and other addictions have reached epidemic proportions in today's society. Christ's intervention in dealing with these issues will not only cure the addicted but also can transform the lives of affected family members and friends. The road to recovery starts with a realization of the problem, earnest prayer, and a reliance on the power of a living and loving God through faith in Christ.

- It pleases God when parents or adult children of elderly parents take care of loved ones who cannot care for themselves. But such caregivers must be careful not to neglect their own needs or health in the process. And they should not succumb to resentment, anger, or hopelessness. God wants us to rely on Him for the comfort, strength, and hope that only He can provide. As Matthew 11:30 says, "For my yoke is easy and my burden is light."

- In times of desperation, don't be reluctant to come boldly to the throne of God and stand on His promises to meet your needs and answer your prayers. Often even strong believers find themselves sheepishly coming to the Lord with their requests. The scriptural promises are stronger than that.

A Prayer for Those Struggling with Family Issues

The stories in this chapter are about crises related to a variety of family issues, including serious illnesses, accidents, addictions, broken relationships, and even gender identity issues. If you are facing any of these issues, here is a prayer that you can modify to reflect your specific situation:

Loving and gracious God, my family and the children you have given me are a blessed gift. Forgive me if I have knowingly or unknowingly done or said anything to fracture those relationships.

Please help me reflect love, tolerance, wisdom, and understanding as I seek healing and reconciliation for those I may have hurt. Use me as a complimentary instrument of your intervention as I pray for the healing of those in our family who are injured or suffering in any way.

Help me provide the loving guidance my family needs without criticizing, lecturing, or judging. Give me the wisdom to know what to say, when to say it, and how to say it. Surround me with the resources and people I need to help me get through this situation.

In Jesus' name I pray. Amen.

7

NAVIGATING GRIEF
RELATED TO LOSS

When a loved one dies, life seems to stop, and the grief can be all-consuming. Images, smells, and sounds can trigger memories that seem to start the grieving process all over again. Losing a parent or a child is especially devastating. These losses redefine the very identities of surviving family members and require that they find a path forward without the most important people in their lives.

The death of a parent is traumatic at any age, but it is especially traumatic for children.

Many people consider the death of a child the most devastating type of loss known to humankind. People typically expect to die before their children do. When a child dies before his or her parents, the loss of that child's future is heartbreaking and difficult to accept.

In 1969, Elisabeth Kübler-Ross, MD, published the book *On Death & Dying*, which became widely acclaimed and accepted as a helpful guide to the stages of grief, which often overlap:

1. Denial and isolation
2. Anger
3. Bargaining
4. Depression
5. Acceptance[1]

Turning to God by praying and reading the Bible can help ease the pain associated with grief. When we accept God's grace, we open ourselves to the comfort He provides us during our times of loss.

> But you, God, see the trouble of the afflicted; you consider their grief and take it in hand. The victims commit themselves to you; you are the helper of the fatherless. (Psalm 10:14)

> Praise be to the God and Father of our Lord Jesus Christ, the Father of compassion and the God of all comfort, who comforts us in all our troubles, so that we can comfort those in any trouble with the comfort we ourselves receive from God. (2 Corinthians 1:3–4)

> Defend the weak and the fatherless; uphold the cause of the poor and the oppressed. (Psalm 82:3)

Spreading Fatherly Love: Helping Grieving Children

Bob Delonti.

Almost one in twenty-five children will experience the death of a parent before age eighteen.[2] One article on the subject explains that "when [a parent's] death occurs during adolescence, it complicates a teenager's natural process of defining his or her identity in the world. The tension between seeking independence and reliance on family support tend to magnify the process of bereavement, according to David E. Balk's 2009 book *Adolescent Encounters with Death, Bereavement, and Coping*. In most cases, teenagers in mourning suffer from low self-esteem."[3] This often makes it difficult for them to maintain healthy relationships, finish college, or

192

enter rewarding careers. Low self-esteem also can lead to depression, self-harm, bullying, and even suicidal tendencies.

According to a long-term study published online by *JAMA Psychiatry*:

> The death of a parent in childhood was associated with a long-term risk of suicide in a study of children from three Scandinavian countries who were followed for up to forty years … In Western societies, 3 to 4 percent of children experience the death of a parent, and it is one of the most stressful and potentially harmful life events in childhood. While most children and adolescents adapt to the loss, others develop preventable social and psychological problems.[4]

To help a child cope with the loss of a parent, here are some tips from Robert Zucker, author of *The Journey Through Grief and Loss: Helping Yourself and Your Child When Grief Is Shared*:

- Be honest and direct about the parent's death, and be informative but not graphic.
- Ask for help from others so that you will have the time, energy, and resources to be there for your child.
- Answer the child's tough questions in honest ways, or else he or she will stop asking them.
- Have your child talk to someone else—an adult who is not grieving.
- Listen without interrupting, and encourage the child to talk about his or her feelings. [5]

In 2 Samuel, we see how David reacted when his child died only seven days after being born:

> David pleaded with God for the child. He fasted and spent the nights lying in sackcloth on the ground. The elders of his household stood beside him to get him up from the ground, but he refused, and he would not eat any food with them. On the seventh day the child died. David's attendants were afraid

to tell him that the child was dead, for they thought, "While the child was still living, he wouldn't listen to us when we spoke to him. How can we now tell him the child is dead? He may do something desperate." David noticed that his attendants were whispering among themselves, and he realized the child was dead. "Is the child dead?" he asked. "Yes," they replied, "he is dead." Then David got up from the ground. After he had washed, put on lotions and changed his clothes, he went into the house of the LORD and worshiped. Then he went to his own house, and at his request they served him food, and he ate. (2 Samuel 12:16–20)

It is certainly natural for a parent to feel angry upon the death of a child. We see in this Scripture that David pleaded with God for his child, and he refused to eat. But once he saw that the child had died, he realized it was God's will, and he "went into the house of the LORD and worshiped." Worshipping God even in the midst of tragedy shows that we have full confidence in His plan for our lives, even if we have difficulty understanding why it happened.

Bob Delonti is a past board member and veteran volunteer for Comfort Zone Camp, an organization that provides support for grieving children who have lost a parent or sibling. Bob has served as a "Big Buddy" mentor in dozens of camps, flying from California at his own expense to attend camps in Virginia and New Jersey. (You can read more about these bereavement camps for children at comfortzonecamp.org.)

Bob cares about these grieving children because he knows how they feel. He lost both of his parents at a young age. Then, as an adult, he lost his stepson. His faith is incredible and an inspiration to anyone who meets him. His wife, Donna, is also remarkable; she has experienced loss as well. She prayed for Bob to experience God's love and saving grace, and her prayers were answered—Bob subsequently found the Lord and later committed to serving Him. This is a great example of God's grace.

Here is Bob's story.

I am sixty years old and have been married to Donna for thirty-four years. I was born in Scranton, Pennsylvania, and currently live in California. Donna and I have a daughter who is forty-seven, and our son died in a motorcycle accident at age twenty-four, in 1991. These are my stepchildren, but I have raised them as my own.

I was raised in the Catholic Church and completed the full spectrum of sacraments, from my first Holy Communion to confirmation. I didn't attend church on a regular basis, though, and I always had questions about God's existence and whereabouts. I never had a personal relationship with Christ.

My Parents' Death

My mother died in March 1972, just six days after my fifteenth birthday, and my father died in July of the same year.

The death of both my parents at age fifteen caused anger, grief, and loneliness that I can't adequately describe in words. Losing the two most important human beings in my life at a time when I most needed them paralyzed me emotionally for many years. After my mother died, I would listen to my father cry each night, and I would pray that they could be together. When he died suddenly a few months later, I struggled under the guilt of those prayers and experienced a crushing void. I cried myself to sleep at night and found it difficult to breathe as I lay in bed, feeling I was suffocating as I choked on the painful lump in my own throat.

As a teenager, I carried insurmountable anger that I tried to release, to no avail, through football, drinking, and fighting. After high school, I escaped to California, where I could no longer be the "kid with no parents," hoping for a fresh start.

I have two siblings—an older brother and a younger sister. I never discussed our parents' death with either of them until years later. After their death, the three of us went to live with relatives nearby, but it wasn't an ideal situation, and it was a poor fit for all parties. My brother, who was twenty at the time, moved out within weeks.

I moved out at the age of seventeen and lived with my brother until moving to California in 1976. I was fully separated from the church by this time.

Donna

When Donna and I began dating in 1982, she asked about my family. I had never talked about my loss, so it was like opening a floodgate. After ten years of hiding, I came face-to-face with my grief. At the time, I didn't recognize that God was at work, but He had a plan. Donna and I married in 1983.

Donna was churched beginning at an early age and had a close personal relationship with Jesus Christ when we married. While she attended American Baptist church services on Sundays, I played golf. I felt guilty at times, thinking Donna wanted me to attend church with her. One day, I asked her why she wasn't more forceful in getting me to go to church. Her response was, "I've been praying for you, but I am responsible for my salvation, and you are responsible for yours."

Our Son's Death

I thought no pain could ever exceed the pain I had felt when my parents died, but I was wrong. The death of our son was the worst experience imaginable. It's every parent's greatest nightmare, but for us the nightmare was a reality. When someone you love deeply and unconditionally, so much so that you'd gladly give your own life to save theirs, dies, the loss is unbearable.

I still considered myself a Catholic but started asking more questions and seeking God. I began attending church on a regular basis while still trying to figure out my spiritual life. One year after our son's death, I accepted Jesus Christ and was baptized soon afterward.

Through persistent prayer and appeals to the Lord for His healing power, I found a peace and calm I never thought possible. I have directly experienced God's grace as I recovered slowly from my grief and discovered a new purpose.

It took me a while to understand that God had been working on me since childhood. My wife and I realize that without the presence of God in our lives, we would never have made it to this point. Since 1992, we have both been active in church ministries (Elder Board, College Bible Study, Children's Ministry, Homeless Ministry, and Church Planting Ministry).

Navigating Grief

In 2001, God led me to Comfort Zone Camp (CZC) through an article in *Guideposts* magazine. It was a perfect match for me, to use my gifts helping children navigate grief. Who better to help young people in need of unconditional love and parental guidance than someone like me who has had exactly the same experience and who had the deeply rooted need to love and nurture a child in need after losing my own son. My experiences, as devastating as they were, found an outlet in helping others which gives me great joy. I thank the Lord daily that my own grief prepared me for a lay ministry to other young people dealing with the loss of a loved one.

Bob says Psalm 91 has become a lifelong source of comfort and strength since the death of his son. He and his wife found a para-phrased version of Psalm 91 in their son's wallet. Bob told me, "He carried it with him at all times, and knowing that he had this reminder with him at the time of his death brought us comfort and peace because we knew that he was secure in his faith."

Whoever dwells in the shelter of the Most High will rest in the shadow of the Almighty. I will say of the LORD, "He is my refuge and my fortress, my God, in whom I trust." Surely he will save you from the fowler's snare and from the deadly pestilence. He will cover you with his feathers, and under his wings you will find refuge; his faithfulness will be your shield and rampart. You will not fear the terror of night, nor the arrow that flies by day, nor the pestilence that stalks in the darkness, nor the plague that destroys at midday. A thousand may fall at your side, ten thousand at your right hand, but it will not come near you. You will only observe with your eyes and see the punishment of the wicked. If you say, "The LORD is my refuge," and you make the Most High your dwelling, no harm will overtake you, no disaster will come near your tent. For he will command his angels concerning you to guard you in all your ways; they will lift you up in their hands, so that you will not strike your foot against a stone. You will tread on the lion and the cobra; you will trample the great lion and the serpent. "Because he loves me," says the LORD, "I will rescue him; I will protect him, for he acknowledges my name. He will call on me, and I will answer him; I will be with him in trouble, I will deliver him and honor him. With long life I will satisfy him and show him my salvation." (Psalm 91:1–16)

Here are two additional verses that have provided Bob with strength during his most difficult times:

For it is by grace that you have been saved, through faith—and this is not from yourselves, it is the gift of God. (Ephesians 2:8)

Not only so, but we also glory in our sufferings, because we know that suffering produces perseverance; perseverance, character; and character, hope. And hope does not put us to shame, because God's love has been poured out into our hearts through the Holy Spirit, who has been given to us. (Romans 5:3–5)

My Thoughts on Bob's Story

It was tragic enough that Bob lost both of his parents when he was fifteen years old, but then when he grew up and got married, his son died. One year after their son's death, Bob accepted Jesus Christ and was baptized soon afterward. Sometimes when tragedies happen, people become angry with God and ask why He would take a loved one from them. Bob's grief brought him closer to God. He said, "Through persistent prayer and appeals to the Lord for His healing power, I found a peace and calm I never thought possible."

Bob's story illustrates how losing a loved one led to "resetting" his life and rediscovering a new purpose. Bob said, "I have directly experienced God's grace as I recovered slowly from my grief and discovered a new purpose." Now, through Comfort Zone Camp, he counsels grieving children who have lost parents. No one can relate to these children like someone who has been in their shoes. Bob sets a wonderful example of someone who asked God to show him how he could pay His grace forward by using the lessons he learned during his own life tragedies to help others who are experiencing similar situations.

Time for Personal Reflection

1. As a child, what types of loss did you experience?

2. To what extent did an adult help you process your grief?

3. How did the experience affect your outlook on life as an adult? To what extent have you come to terms with this grief?

4. Sometimes, our grief is more intense if we did not get a chance to say good-bye to our loved one. Consider writing a letter to your lost loved one now, telling that person how much you loved him or her and what he or she meant to you. This very specific act can sometimes help us heal from the grief associated with loss.

Heavenly Messages:
After My Daughter's Death

The day after her daughter Liz's funeral, Kim's sister-in-law
brought her this photo of the Wencl cousins taken during
Christmas 2002. In it, Liz (with her young cousin on her lap)
is wearing khaki pants and a light-blue sweater–the same
type of clothes Kim had bought for Liz to be buried in.
In the store at the mall a few days earlier, Kim had silently
asked her then-deceased daughter, Liz, to guide her
in choosing the clothing–and she did.

Kimberly Wencl of Owatonna, Minnesota, is a sixty-three-year-old
wife and mother who worked in the business world for thirty-five
years before retiring in 2009. She and her husband, Roger, have a
thirty-one-year-old daughter, Anna. Their older daughter, Elizabeth
(Liz), was three years older than Anna. In 2003, when Liz was in college, she died in a house fire after moving into the off-campus house
only three weeks earlier.

Since Liz's death fourteen years ago, Kim has been comforted by
the knowledge that Liz is always with her. Kim has received several
precious "messages from beyond" that assure her of Liz's everlast-
ing presence in her life. Kim believes that "Love never dies, and the
bond we all share with those we love is never broken ... not even by
death!" This is Kim's story.

I was numb as I sat in the chair between my husband and my father. I could hear the funeral director talking … I could see his lips moving, but nothing was registering in my mind. Even breathing was difficult. In the previous twenty-four hours, life as we knew it had ceased to exist. Our oldest daughter, twenty-year-old Elizabeth, had died of smoke inhalation from a fire in her duplex just a few blocks from the University of Minnesota, where she had just begun her sophomore year. Two of her roommates also died.

Part of me—no, all of me—wanted to scream and run out of the room, go home and find my beautiful, precious Elizabeth, safe in her room. She would look at me with that coy smile of hers and say, "Oh, Mom, you just worry way too much! Nothing is going to happen to me. I'm just fine!"

Liz's Spirit

The funeral director gently told us that we would need to bring in clothing for Liz to be buried in. There was no hurry, he said, but in the next day or two. As his words began to slowly sink in, I mentally scanned Liz's closet—and it was empty. She had taken everything with her when she moved into that duplex just three weeks earlier.

The harsh reality was that I would have to go out and buy Liz an outfit to be buried in—one last, final new outfit. She always loved to shop, and she loved new clothes, so it seemed fitting that a new outfit was needed for this occasion as well. But how could I shop without her? We never agreed on clothing, and now in this difficult, painful state of mind, I had to pick out her final new outfit?

My sister drove me to the mall. I knew I would go to a store where Liz used to work because she had always liked the clothes there. As I pulled open the door and stepped inside, I whispered, "Liz, you have got to help me here! I have absolutely no idea what to pick."

I slowly walked around and began to peruse the racks. It didn't take very long before I found a pair of khaki pants and a light blue sweater. I showed my sister and said, "I don't know if this is what Liz would want, but even if I don't get this right, does it really matter?"

A day after the funeral, my sister-in-law came to visit. We sat in my kitchen drinking coffee and talking. The grim reality that Elizabeth was gone had begun to sink in.

"I was going through pictures last night," Karen told me, "and I found one of Liz taken last Christmas. I thought you might want to see it."

She reached into her purse, pulled out a picture, and set it on the table in front of me. There she was—my Elizabeth, smiling and happy, sitting with her cousins. Suddenly my breath caught in my throat, and I couldn't speak. In the photo, Liz was wearing a pair of khaki pants and a light blue sweater! This confirmation of Liz's presence with me was a gift of grace from God.

A Pre-Death Letter

Three weeks after Liz's death, I took a job working with the international customers at a locally owned, family-based automotive tool company. Because of the time differences, email was their accepted means of communication. It was the perfect job for me; the stress level was low. I could go in, answer the emails I received, and go home. I thanked God often for giving me such a wonderful job at just the right time.

I continued to work through my emails. Suddenly, a familiar email address popped up. It was Liz's high school French teacher, Jan. She had been Liz's favorite teacher, and we had kept in touch after her death. Here is what Jan wrote:

Kim,

You will just treasure this. I was in my classroom yesterday, cleaning out my files, getting ready for a new school year. A lone file folder fell on the floor. I reached down and picked it up, and on the outside it was labeled "Liz Wencl Essay." I opened it up and discovered an assignment I had given out more than four years ago.

The assignment was to write a letter to one of your parents, in French, telling them what they represent in your life. Kim, this is a letter Liz wrote to you!

I don't speak French, so Jan translated it for me. That letter was a parent's dream. In it Liz told me how much she loved and missed me in so many different ways. And, amazingly, even though the letter was written when she was in high school, it made complete sense for life after September 20, 2003. Here is the English translation of the letter:

Dear Mom,

I know that you love me. You show me each day that it is true. Don't think you are a bad mother. It isn't true! When I look at you, I realize how much I am loved.

When you are feeling bad, don't forget—I truly love you. I would like to be a better daughter. We argue sometimes, and that makes me sad. I feel bad and unhappy if you cry.

I remember when I was little and you would hug me and say, "I love you so much, Lizzie. Sit here with me for just a little while." Those times were so special for me, and you made me so happy. I felt like nothing could ever hurt me. I used to wish those moments would never end. To be cuddled up next to you like that today would be like a dream come true.

Mom, I feel sad when you feel sad. And, when you are happy, I am happy! You are my mother, and I would never choose anyone else. Without you, I would never be who I am.

I love you with all my heart.

Kisses,

Liz

I emailed all my friends and family members to share this wonderful letter with them.

Jan brought the folder and the letter to my house that night. As she put them in my hands, she said to me, "You have got to know this was no accident." I said, "Oh, Jan, believe me, I do know that."

She went on to tell me that she remembered telling Liz what a beautiful letter it was and encouraging Liz to share it with me. She remembered what Liz's comment had been: "I will when the time is right."

Receiving that letter was no coincidence. I believe with all my heart that my daughter is still with me. She reached out to let me know just how much she loves and misses me, just as I love and miss her.

The letter is now framed, with the French version on one side, a picture of Liz in the middle, and the English translation on the other. It hangs in our living room, a constant reminder of the power of our love. Just as God's love for his children never changes, the love that my daughter and I share never changes. It is a gift of grace from God and will live for all eternity.

A Gift for Grandpa

In February 2012, eight years after Liz's death, my family planned a get-together at a local restaurant to celebrate my dad's eightieth birthday. Dad doesn't like a lot of fuss, but he good-naturedly went along with all our plans.

I had managed to get his birthday celebration on our local 10:00 p.m. news, and many people let Dad know they had seen it. A picture of Dad was in that day's newspaper announcing his milestone birthday. And there were flowers on the altar at church … all in honor of Dad.

We somehow managed to get our own private room for our dinner. We were free to talk and laugh and carry on without disturbing anyone. Two of my favorite cousins, Dawn and Beth, were there. They loved my dad and were very close to him. As we finished our meal with an extravagant chocolate dessert, we all raised our glasses and toasted Dad. He smiled from ear to ear and got a little teary as he told us how proud he was of his family and how much he loved us.

Beth worked for a photographer, who busily snapped photos throughout our time at the restaurant. As we got ready to leave, we all stood proudly around Dad and took a family photo—something we had not done for a very long time.

Despite the happiness of the day, I couldn't help but be sad. "If only Elizabeth were here," I thought. "Then this day would be perfect." There would always be an empty chair at our family table that no one but Elizabeth could fill.

The next day, I received an email from Beth thanking me for inviting her. She included some of the photos she had taken. She wrote, "I was concerned when I downloaded the photos and brought the first one up, only to see a large white spot just above your head, on your husband's arm." Beth was dismayed and wondered how this could have happened. Would this spot ruin all the pictures? Beth observed that none of the other photos had this white orb, or circle, on them. She concluded that quite possibly this was a visit from Liz.

When Beth showed the photo to me, I knew that it was indeed Liz's presence with us, showing up in the photo. What a wonderful gift Liz had given to her family, especially her Grandpa! I printed the photo and excitedly asked my dad to stop by. "I have one last gift for you," I told him.

When he came into my kitchen later that day, he gently scolded me: "Kimmie, I don't need any more birthday presents! Everything you gave me yesterday was wonderful."

I said, "Oh, I think you'll want this one, Dad. But you'd better sit down first."

This is the only photo from the 80th-birthday celebration for Kim's dad in which a white orb appears right above Kim's head. She said, "That is exactly where Liz would have stood." Kim believes this is visual proof that she was with the family that day.

When I put the photo down in front of Dad, he stared at it for a few minutes. Then he was overcome with emotion as he realized the significance of the white spot. We both shed tears of joy at the thought that our beloved Elizabeth had been with us the previous day on such a special occasion.

By the grace of God, love never dies, and the bond we all share with those we love is never broken ... not even by death!

Honoring Liz's Memory

Because of the marvelous gifts of God's loving grace that allowed us to reconnect with Liz in our times of grief and celebration, I was eager to return God's grace to others. Very early on after Liz's death, I decided that the best way to honor her life was for me to live my best life—to love, to laugh, and to serve others. I have done that in several ways.

Every opportunity I get, I speak to audiences and share what I call "Tragedy to Transformation—A Mother's Story." I also work behind the scenes at our local Compassionate Friends grief group, serve as a hospice volunteer, and serve in many different ways at my church.

I reach out to those who lose a child and offer my sympathies. Often I meet with them one-on-one to listen and to be present with them as they begin their journey.

Back in 2007, I started a blog called "Love Lives On."[6] In it, I share my stories of my continued connection to my daughter. I wrote a piece five years ago and recently got a Facebook reminder about it. When I read it again, I really had no recollection of writing it. It felt very profound. I believe with all my heart that these words are not my words but come from the God of the universe.

The following are Bible verses Kim says she turns to when she misses Liz the most. John 8:7 was Liz's "life verse" that she chose when being confirmed. These verses reinforce the presence of God's grace in our lives as we make our journey through the profound loss of our loved ones:

When they kept on questioning him, he straightened up and said to them, "Let any one of you who is without sin be the first to throw a stone at her." (John 8:7)

Jesus said to her, "I am the resurrection and the life. The one who believes in me will live, even though they die." (John 11:25)

No, in all these things we are more than conquerors through him who loved us. For I am convinced that neither death nor life, neither angels nor demons, neither the present nor the future, nor any powers, neither height nor depth, nor anything else in all creation, will be able to separate us from the love of God that is in Christ Jesus our Lord. (Romans 8:37–39)

My Thoughts on Kim's Story

I admire Kim for being so open to the signs and symbols of Liz's presence since she died. Kim reminds us how powerful our love for one another can be. She said, "Love never dies, and the bond we all share with those we love is never broken ... not even by death!"

Kim's story demonstrates that losing a loved one tragically can also provide an opportunity to honor that person's life in service to others. She said, "Very early on after Liz's death, I decided that the best way to honor her life was for me to live my best life—to love, to laugh, and to serve others." And she is doing just that by providing support and comfort to other parents who have lost children, through the presentation she gives called "Tragedy to Transformation—A Mother's Story."

Time for Personal Reflection

1. When you have lost loved ones, what did you do to relieve the grief? Did you bury your pain, or did you seek solace in the comfort of God's Word and in prayer? Did you seek out compassionate people who had a similar experience?

Looking back on it now, what else could you have done to bring comfort to yourself and to your family?

2. Do you believe that your loved ones who have passed on are still with you? What types of phenomena have you experienced that you consider proof of them being with you? Have you ever experienced treasured "messages from beyond," as Kim did after the death of her daughter?

3. How would you comfort a close friend who is struggling with unresolved grief?

Healing Insights

- The people in our lives are cherished gifts from God, and we do not know how long we will have with them. When God takes a beloved parent, child, or other loved one home to be with Him, the loss is devastating, and the grief never goes away. We cannot easily "move on" from the death of a loved one. Instead, we must go through the natural grieving process, seek the comfort of those around us, and relearn how to relate to God and the world around us without our loved one in our presence.

- After a loved one dies, we can look for signs that his or her spirit is still with us. Those signs can bring us comfort and joy in the midst of our grief.

- Worshipping God after the death of a loved one may seem impossible to do. But when we follow David's example from the book of 2 Samuel and do just that, we are acknowledging that the loss may be part of God's plan and that He is in control. Nehemiah 8:10 says, "Do not grieve, for the joy of the LORD is your strength."

- The void we fill after a significant loss can stay with us for the rest of our lives. Claiming God's grace and forgiveness, and knowing we will see loved ones in heaven again one day, provides comfort.

- If you feel, or if someone you know feels that the grief is not subsiding, consider reaching out to one of these reputable organizations for help:

  » Depression and Bipolar Support Alliance (DBSA), 800-826-3632, dbsalliance.org

  » National Alliance on Mental Illness (NAMI), 800-950-6264, nami.org

  » National Institute of Mental Health (NIMH), 866-615-6464, nimh.nih.gov

  » Mental Health America (MHA—formerly known as the National Mental Health Association, NMHA), 800-273-8255, mentalhealthamerica.net

A Prayer for Those Struggling with Grief as a Result of Loss

The stories in this chapter are about crises related to grief following the loss of a parent or child. If you are grieving the loss of a loved one, here is a prayer for you to modify as appropriate for your situation:

Heavenly Father, You brought _____ into my life, and I am so very grateful for the time we had together here on Earth, even though it is devastating to me that we did not get more time together. It feels as though this debilitating sense of loss will never go away. Please give me strength to go on without him/her. Please help me find a renewed sense of meaning in life without _____'s presence.

I know there is a reason for everything, and I know You welcome each one of us believers into your presence when it is time. It is so hard for me to understand and to cope with this tragic loss, given the limitations of my human reasoning ability. Please cloak me in Your love, compassion, and care. Heal my wounded soul and help me put one foot in front of the other until I learn to "walk" again in this new phase of my life.

Please show me how to honor _____'s memory in a way that is healing to me and respectful to his/her legacy. And please send me signs and symbols of his/her presence to remind me that he/she is still with me.

In Jesus' name I pray. Amen.

8

YOUR ACCESS
TO GRACE—
ASSURANCES FROM JESUS

This chapter summarizes the key elements common among the stories told in this book that resulted in the individuals in crisis developing a deeper relationship with Christ and an outpouring of God's grace. That realization of God's grace provided each of them with relief from their crisis and a desire to return that grace to others in Christian service.

It struck me as I was writing and editing the early drafts of the contributors' stories that, despite the significant variations in their individual situations, there are some common instructive elements that readers can take away in their personal quests to overcome similar crises.

In general terms, the following pattern seems to be almost universally present in the contributors' stories, demonstrating how they not only experienced God's grace but did so in a way that profoundly transformed them and caused them to find ways to give back to others out of their extreme gratitude.

As noted in the preface, the Christian experience many times progresses through the following three phases:

1. Experiencing a crisis
2. Receiving grace (either prevenient, justifying, or both)
3. Returning grace (i.e., sanctifying grace) to others

Most of the inspiring and compelling stories in this book reflect all three of the above phases. These are stories of individuals who were in a crisis, either of their own volition or imposed on them by external influences. Whatever their particular crisis, they all cried out to the Lord for help.

Now that you've had the benefit of reading about these grace-filled experiences, I want to illuminate the common threads among the stories. This will highlight the process for emerging triumphantly through crises and enable you to identify the best practices that knowingly or unknowingly contributed to these remarkable true stories of renewal and recovery.

This is not meant to provide a recipe for a guaranteed blessing of God's grace, or even a template for recovering from a crisis. God works at times in His own mysterious ways and according to His own perfect timing. Nonetheless, identifying common elements will provide you with potentially stronger insights and may even offer guidance on how you might respond to your own situation or how you may assist others in their struggles. Most importantly, in the notes for Phase 2, I explore the very words of Jesus to provide reassurances about access to His loving grace.

Phase 1: Experiencing a Crisis

All people face challenges and crises in their lives. Everyone who shared their story in this book was in despair. Nothing they seemed to do provided them the relief they desired, that is, until they turned to God in their desperation.

The particularities of each case were quite different. This is evident in the chapter structure of the book, which covers a broad spectrum of afflictions. Whether their crisis was due to abuse, addiction, emotional or physical pain, work pressures, family dysfunction, or devastating losses, they all found relief in God's unmerited grace.

God's grace is not easily definable, but as the experiences of those who tell their stories in this book illustrate, grace was revealed to them in dramatic and undeniable ways. In most cases, they were instantly and powerfully aware of God's outpouring of His loving grace.

Phase 2: Receiving Grace

There is no cookie-cutter approach for receiving God's grace, but there are revealing elements of commonality in many of the stories in this book. Dozens of inspiring scriptural verses are referenced by those who relied on them at various stages of their crises and recoveries. They come from both the Old Testament and the New Testament.

I made a conscious decision not to remove some of the redundant references to the same Scripture within multiple stories. Each contributor has his or her own favorites, and seeing a verse or passage appear multiple times is supporting evidence of its power in reassuring those who relied on it.

To buttress what you have already experienced in reading chapters 1 through 7, I have identified from the Gospels what Jesus Himself said that is relevant to the commonalities in many of the stories in this book.

Some of the more common attributes and practices of those who received an outpouring of God's grace in these stories can be summarized in the following four ways. It is important to note that it is not necessary for all of these attributes to be present to receive grace. For example, prevenient grace as theorized by John Wesley (and as I personally experienced) precedes a strong and persistent faith in Jesus.

Nonetheless, one or more of these four attributes seems to exist in every story in the book:

1. Strong and persistent faith in Jesus Christ
2. Reliance on comforting Scripture

3. Frequent and often bold prayers
4. Forgiveness of others

Consider what Jesus said directly or indirectly about each of these topics.

A. Strong and Persistent Faith in Jesus Christ

The gospel of John is the most theological book of the four gospels. In it, the disciple John is most concerned with convincing readers of the deity of Christ and then confirming that deity by recounting the many miracles that Christ performed for the benefit of those of genuine faith. So it is no surprise that you'll find an abundance of Jesus' own words and stories of healing in this book. (It's easy to understand why, in Bob Uber's story in chapter 4, his mother had him distribute the Vietnamese translations of the gospel of John during his Vietnam War experience).

Jesus' words and the biblical recounting of His many miracles reinforces my faith and can do the same for you.

1. *Here is just a small sampling of verses in which Jesus reveals who He is:*

I am the resurrection and the life. The one who believes in me will live, even though they die; and whoever lives by believing in me will never die. (John 11:25–26)

When Jesus spoke again to the people, he said, "I am the light of the world. Whoever follows me will never walk in darkness, but will have the light of life." (John 8:12)

I and the Father are one. (John 10:30)

You call me "Teacher" and "Lord," and rightly so, for that is what I am. (John 13:13)

Then he called the crowd to him along with his disciples and said: "Whoever wants to be my disciple must deny

themselves and take up their cross and follow me. For whoever wants to save their life will lose it, but whoever loses
their life for me and for the gospel will save it. What good
is it for someone to gain the whole world, yet forfeit their
soul? Or what can anyone give in exchange for their soul?"
(Mark 8:34–37)

Jesus answered: "Don't you know me, Philip, even after I have
been among you such a long time? Anyone who has seen me
has seen the Father. How can you say, 'Show us the Father'?
Don't you believe that I am in the Father, and that the Father
is in me?" (John 14:9–10)

2. *Numerous stories of miracles in the Gospels often appear in
   two, three, or even all four of the gospel accounts. In the vast
   majority of these, Jesus indicates that it was through faith
   that those in need were healed.*

The following are just a few of the biblical stories of Christ's heal-
ings in which He explicitly mentions the importance of the recipient's
faith:

- Jesus heals a centurion's servant (Matthew 8:5–13, Luke
  7:1–10)

- Jesus heals a paralytic (Matthew 9:1–8, Mark 2:1–12, Luke
  5:17–26)

- Jesus heals a woman in the crowd (Matthew 9:20–22,
  Mark 5:25–34, Luke 8:42–48)

- Jesus heals two blind men (Matthew 9:27–31)

- Jesus heals a demon-possessed daughter (Matthew 15:21–
  28, Mark 7:24–30)

- Jesus heals a boy possessed by a demon (Matthew 17:14–
  20, Mark 9:14–29, Luke 9:37–43)

- Jesus raises Lazarus from the dead (John 11:1–45)

Here is just one such story from the gospel of Luke in which Jesus heals the woman in a crowd who had suffered from bleeding for twelve years. She was instantly healed after touching His cloak. Her hesitancy and fear is easy to understand because she was considered unclean, as was anyone she touched.

> As Jesus was on his way, the crowds almost crushed him. And a woman was there who had been subject to bleeding for twelve years, but no one could heal her. She came up behind him and touched the edge of his cloak, and immediately her bleeding stopped. "Who touched me?" Jesus asked. When they all denied it, Peter said, "Master, the people are crowding and pressing against you." But Jesus said, "Someone touched me; I know that power has gone out from me." Then the woman, seeing that she could not go unnoticed, came trembling and fell at his feet. In the presence of all the people, she told why she had touched him and how she had been instantly healed. Then he said to her, "Daughter, your faith has healed you. Go in peace." (Luke 8:42–48)

B. Reliance on Comforting Scripture

Many of those who tell their stories in this book relied on and often repeated to themselves comforting verses from the Bible. People of faith rely on the words of Jesus for reassurance when they experience significant challenges or crises in their lives. This is a small collection of such heartwarming and encouraging verses:

> Blessed are those who mourn, for they will be comforted. (Matthew 5:4)

> Now is your time of grief, but I will see you again and you will rejoice, and no one will take away your joy. (John 16:22)

> Come to me, all you who are weary and burdened, and I will give you rest. Take my yoke upon you and learn from me, for I am gentle and humble in heart, and you will find rest

for your souls. For my yoke is easy and my burden is light. (Matthew 11:28–30)

I have told you these things, so that in me you may have peace. In this world you will have trouble. But take heart! I have overcome the world. (John 16:33)

Therefore do not worry about tomorrow, for tomorrow will worry about itself. Each day has enough trouble of its own. (Matthew 6:34)

For the bread of God is he who comes down from heaven and gives life to the world.... I am the bread of life. He who comes to me will never go hungry, and he who believes in me will never be thirsty. (John 6:33, 35)

But the Advocate, the Holy Spirit, whom the Father will send in my name, will teach you all things and will remind you of everything I have said to you. Peace I leave with you; my peace I give you. I do not give to you as the world gives. Do not let your hearts be troubled and do not be afraid. (John 14:26–27)

C. Frequent and Often Bold Prayers

The four gospels of Matthew, Mark, Luke, and John speak often of Jesus' prayer life and what he taught them about prayer. The following are some relevant Scripture passages.

2. *Jesus set an example by praying often:*

But Jesus often withdrew to lonely places and prayed. (Luke 5:16)

One of those days Jesus went out to a mountainside to pray, and spent the night praying to God. (Luke 6:12)

About eight days after Jesus said this, he took Peter, John and James with him and went up onto a mountain to pray. (Luke 9:28)

Righteous Father, though the world does not know you, I know you, and they know that you have sent me. I have made you known to them, and will continue to make you known in order that the love you have for me may be in them and that I myself may be in them. (John 17:25–26)

Going a little farther, he fell with his face to the ground and prayed, "My Father, if it is possible, may this cup be taken from me. Yet not as I will, but as you will." (Matthew 26:39)

He went away a second time and prayed, "My Father, if it is not possible for this cup to be taken away unless I drink it, may your will be done." (Matthew 26:42)

Jesus said, "Father, forgive them, for they do not know what they are doing." (Luke 23:34)

3. *Jesus taught the faithful how to pray:*

This, then, is how you should pray: "Our Father in heaven, hallowed be your name, your kingdom come, your will be done, on earth as it is in heaven. Give us today our daily bread. And forgive us our debts, as we also have forgiven our debtors. And lead us not into temptation, but deliver us from the evil one." (Matthew 6:9–13)

3. *Jesus provides reassurance that He is listening:*

For where two or three gather in my name, there am I with them. (Matthew 18:20)

Ask and it will be given to you; seek and you will find; knock and the door will be opened to you. For everyone who asks receives; the one who seeks finds; and to the one who knocks, the door will be opened. (Matthew 7:7–8)

4. *Jesus talked about the power of prayer:*

Which of you fathers, if your son asks for a fish, will give him a snake instead? Or if he asks for an egg, will give him a scorpion? If you then, though you are evil, know how to give good gifts to your children, how much more will your Father in heaven give the Holy Spirit to those who ask him! (Luke 11:11–13)

Watch and pray so that you will not fall into temptation. The spirit is willing, but the flesh is weak. (Matthew 26:41)

But to you who are listening I say: Love your enemies, do good to those who hate you, bless those who curse you, pray for those who mistreat you. (Luke 6:27–28)

D. Forgiveness of Others

5. *Jesus taught about forgiveness:*

Do not judge, and you will not be judged. Do not condemn, and you will not be condemned. Forgive, and you will be forgiven. (Luke 6:37)

Then Peter came to Jesus and asked, "Lord, how many times shall I forgive my brother or sister who sins against me? Up to seven times?" Jesus answered, "I tell you, not seven times, but seventy-seven times." (Matthew 18:21–22)

And when you stand praying, if you hold anything against anyone, forgive them, so that your Father in heaven may forgive you your sins. (Mark 11:25)

For if you forgive other people when they sin against you, your heavenly Father will also forgive you. But if you do not forgive others their sins, your Father will not forgive your sins. (Matthew 6:14–15)

Phase 3: Returning Grace to Others

When people are touched by God's grace in a way that is undeniable, as is the case for the contributors of the stories in this book, they are eternally grateful and want others to know that they have access to the same unconditional divine love. It's the power of God's grace in my life that triggered the writing of my first book (*God Revealed*) and then encouraged me to tell the stories of so many others who have shared their love of the Lord and His remarkable impact on their own lives as they faced some of life's most difficult challenges.

The enduring commitment to serve the Lord by those who contributed stories to this book confirms the power of God's grace in their lives and the veracity of their stories. Their lives were literally transformed by God's grace in a way that is glorifying God and impacting many other souls.

⸎

Whatever your personal crisis or challenge, I encourage you to read and reread the often-common elements of these wonderful stories. Choose, reread often, and even memorize some of the scriptural passages to fortify your faith and provide you with hope. Commit to a daily prayer life that will give you quiet time with God and deepen your relationship with Jesus Christ.

Chapters 2 through 7 all end with a prayer you can modify to reflect your own circumstances. And as difficult as it may be, pray as Jesus tells us to pray for your enemies and for those who may have perpetrated unspeakable injustices and crimes against you. Forgive them, and free yourself from the bondage of your own anger and hatred. I am confident that the Lord will reward you for your persistence and your Christian response. Soon you will find yourself recovering from your crisis and entering Phase 3—expressing your own deep gratitude through Christian service to others.

ACKNOWLEDGMENTS

F irst and foremost, I must gratefully acknowledge the courageous contributors of stories to this book. My first book, *God Revealed: Revisit Your Past to Enrich Your Future*, recounted stories of my personal encounters with God over the course of my life in an effort to trigger readers' memories of their own encounters with God.

Those who contributed to the stories of this book were all in crisis and in desperate need of healing or relief. Many of them deeply regretted their own sinful behaviors and found it painful to talk about their situations openly. It was their faith in Jesus Christ and the confidence they had in the guidance of the Holy Spirit that allowed them to joyfully and gratefully share with me, and ultimately with you, the experience of God's grace in their lives and how they were transformed by it. To each of them I owe a deep sense of gratitude, knowing that for them there is great satisfaction in sharing their stories, thereby blessing and impacting many thousands of readers. In doing so, they have pleased God and will certainly be richly blessed.

The support and encouragement of my immediate family and friends, too numerous to mention by name, is what inspired me to complete this book in the face of many other priorities and pursuits.

This book is a culmination of much work by an entire team of extremely competent individuals who made my work much easier and more enjoyable. Social media expert Rebecca Ryan significantly expanded my platform and worked tirelessly to build my following while simultaneously revamping and relaunching our much-improved website, StoriesofGodsGrace.com.

Writer, researcher, and editor Libbye Morris skillfully assisted the book's contributors and me in succinctly and effectively telling their compelling stories in a way that touches all of us deeply.

In addition to the many friends and clergy who reviewed the manuscript, I must thank and make special mention of psychiatrist Dr. Susan Turner, the Reverend Joanne Swenson, the Reverend Harold (Skip) Masback, and ethicist and author Laura Nash, whose insights were very thorough and helpful.

I must also thank literary consultant David Sanford for his invaluable assistance in framing my book proposal and Greg Johnson of Wordserve Literary for suggesting numerous refinements to the manuscript and then effectively pitching the market attractiveness of these stories of God's grace to publishers.

And finally, I am grateful to all the fine folks at BroadStreet Publishing for providing service levels becoming increasingly less common among publishers to facilitate the dissemination of these inspiring and potentially life-changing examples of God's amazing grace. They clearly understand the power of spiritual sharing and personal testimonies.

ABOUT THE AUTHOR

Frederick J. Sievert
Author, Speaker, Retired President
of New York Life Insurance Company,
and Disciple of Christ.

Fred Sievert started his career as a teacher, later entered the insurance business, and retired in 2007 as president of New York Life Insurance Company, a Fortune 100 corporation. Following his retirement at age fifty-nine, Fred attended Yale Divinity School and was awarded a master's degree in 2011.

In his career, Fred enjoyed many successes but also had to deal with much stress, many challenges, and even some serious setbacks. Through it all, he credits his success to a reliance on daily prayer, the guidance of the Holy Spirit, and his relationship with Jesus Christ.

Fred has had many nonfiction essays and articles published in the past, most often about his own providential and life-changing encounters with God. In 2014, he published his first book, *God Revealed: Revisit Your Past to Enrich Your Future*.

He views his thirty-five-year business career as a mere prologue to what God is calling him to do today—write and speak about his faith.

Throughout his adult life, Fred has been active in his church and has served in numerous lay leadership positions. He and his wife, Susan, have five grown children and three granddaughters and reside in East Falmouth, Massachusetts.

You are welcome to connect with Fred Sievert through any of these ways:

Facebook: @fredsiev1

Twitter: @godrevealed

Email: fred@storiesofgodsgrace.com

NOTES

Chapter 1

1 Justin Holcomb, "What Is Grace?" Christianity.com, http://www
.christianity.com/theology/what-is-grace.html.

2 Max Lucado, "God's Grace Is All We Need," August 10, 2013, Faith-
Gateway, http://www.faithgateway.com/gods-grace-is-all-we-need/#.
WY8vVdGQzIU.

3 "Distinctive Wesleyan Doctrines," website of the First United Methodist
Church of Wichita Falls, Texas, http://www.fumcwf.org/wesleyan
-doctrines/.

4 *United Methodist Book of Discipline*, part 2: "Doctrinal Standards," 2016:
52, Cokesbury, https://www.cokesbury.com/forms/Dynamic
Content.aspx?id=87&pageid=920#9568: https://www.scribd.com
/document/35973623/United-Methodist-Book-of-Discipline-part-2
-Doctrinal-Standards.

5 Ibid.

6 Ibid, 53.

7 Rick Warren, "Grace Is Free, but It's Not Cheap," Crosswalk.com, March
9, 2016, http://www.crosswalk.com/devotionals/daily-hope
-with-rick-warren/grace-is-free-but-it-s-not-cheap-daily-hope-with
-rick-warren-march-9-2016.html.

8 Rick Warren, "You Are Saved for a Purpose," *Pastor Rick's Daily Hope*,
March 3, 2016, http://pastorrick.com/devotional/english/you-are-saved
-for-a-purpose.

Chapter 2

1 Olga Khazan, "The Second Assault," *The Atlantic*, December 15, 2015,
http://www.theatlantic.com/health/archive/2015/12/sexual-abuse
-victims-obesity/420186/.

2 "What Are the Statistics of the Abused?" National Association of
Adult Survivors of Child Abuse website, http://www.naasca.org/2012
-Resources/010812-StaisticsOfChildAbuse.htm.

3 "Child Abuse Statistics," American Society for the Positive Care of Children, http://americanspcc.org/child-abuse-statistics/.

4 "Impact of Child Abuse," Adults Surviving Child Abuse, http://www.asca.org.au/WHAT-WE-DO/Resources/General-Information/Impact-of-child-abuse.

5 "Children and Teens: Statistics," RAINN website, https://www.rainn.org/statistics/children-and-teens.

Chapter 3

1 "Understanding Addiction: Professionals' Definitions of 'Addiction,'" Maryland Addiction Recovery Center, December 15, 2015, http://www.marylandaddictionrecovery.com/understanding-addiction-definitions-of-addiction.

2 National Institute on Drug Abuse website, "DrugFacts: Nationwide Trends," https://www.drugabuse.gov/publications/drugfacts/nationwide-trends. The Substance Abuse and Mental Health Services Administration (SAMHSA) conducts the annual National Survey on Drug Use and Health (NSDUH), a major source of information on substance use, abuse, and dependence among Americans who are twelve years of age and older. This data is from 2013, the most recent survey available.

3 Ibid.

4 See conbody.com.

5 See defyventures.org.

6 Christopher Ingraham, "Americans Are Drinking Themselves to Death at Record Rates," *The Washington Post* website, December 22, 2015, https://www.washingtonpost.com/news/wonk/wp/2015/12/22/americans-are-drinking-themselves-to-death-at-record-rates/.

7 "Why Is Alcoholism Classified as a Mental Illness?" Hazelden Betty Ford Foundation, http://www.hazeldenbettyford.org/articles/why-is-alcoholism-classified-as-a-mental-illness.

Chapter 4

1 Alyssa Brown, "Chronic Pain Rates Shoot Up Until Americans Reach Late 50s," Gallup, April 27, 2012, http://www.gallup.com/poll/154169/chronic-pain-rates-shoot-until-americans-reach-late-50s.aspx.

2 Guy Winch, PhD, "Five Ways Emotional Pain Is Worse than Physical Pain," *Psychology Today*, July 20, 2014, https://www.psychologytoday.com/blog/the-squeaky-wheel/201407/5-ways-emotional-pain-is-worse-physical-pain.

3   Emily Brandon, "Study: Delaying Retirement Might Help You Live Longer," *US News & World Report*, May 13, 2016, http://money.usnews.com/money/blogs/planning-to-retire/articles/2016-05-13/study-delaying-retirement-might-help-you-live-longer.

4   "Post-Traumatic Stress Disorder," NIH National Institute of Mental Health, https://www.nimh.nih.gov/health/topics/anxiety-disorders/post-traumatic-stress-disorder.shtml. See also https://medlineplus.gov/magazine/issues/winter09/articles/winter09pg10-14.html.

5   "How Common Is PTSD?" National Center for PTSD, US Veterans Administration, http://www.ptsd.va.gov/public/PTSD-overview/basics/how-common-is-ptsd.asp.

6   "US Breast Cancer Statistics," Breastcancer.org, http://www.breastcancer.org/symptoms/understand_bc/statistics.

7   "Definitions of Recurrent and Metastatic Breast Cancer," Breastcancer.org, http://www.breastcancer.org/symptoms/types/recur_metast/definitions.

8   "Stages of Breast Cancer," Breastcancer.org, http://www.breastcancer.org/symptoms/diagnosis/staging#stage0.

9   "Aortic Aneurysm—Topic Overview," WebMD, http://www.webmd.com/heart-disease/tc/aortic-aneurysm-overview#1.

10 Ibid.

11 "About Chronic Kidney Disease," National Kidney Foundation, https://www.kidney.org/atoz/content/about-chronic-kidney-disease.

12 Ibid.

13 "The Long-Term Effects of Untreated Chronic Pain," Integrative Pain Center of Arizona, http://www.ipcaz.org/long-term-effects-untreated-chronic-pain/.

Chapter 5

1   Joe Folkman and Jack Zenger, "The Riddle of Executives' Ethical Lapses: Can Senior Leadership's Misconduct Be Cured?" Zenger Folkman, http://zengerfolkman.com/wp-content/uploads/2013/05/ZF-The-Riddle-of-Executives-Ethical-Lapses.pdf.

2   Ibid.

3   Steve Bates, "Report Predicts Surge in Workplace Ethical Lapses," Society for Human Resource Management, January 13, 2012, https://www.shrm.org/resourcesandtools/hr-topics/behavioral-competencies/ethical-practice/pages/surgeethicallapses.aspx.

4   Ibid.

5 Ibid.

6 Barbara Bradley Hagerty, "Quit Your Job," *The Atlantic*, April 2016, https://www.theatlantic.com/magazine/archive/2016/04/quit-your-job/471501/.

7 Ibid.

Chapter 6

1 "Seizures in Children," WebMD, http://www.webmd.com/epilepsy/guide/epilepsy-in-children.

2 "Opioid Addiction 2016 Facts & Figures," American Society of Addiction Medicine, http://www.asam.org/docs/default-source/advocacy/opioid-addiction-disease-facts-figures.pdf.

3 Ibid.

4 Lindsey Cook, "The Heroin Epidemic, in Nine Graphs," *US News & World Report*, August 19, 2015, http://www.usnews.com/news/blogs/data-mine/2015/08/19/the-heroin-epidemic-in-9-graphs.

5 "Addiction Medicine: Closing the Gap Between Science and Practice," The National Center on Addiction and Substance Abuse at Columbia University, June 2012, https://www.centeronaddiction.org/addiction-research/reports/addiction-medicine-closing-gap-between-science-and-practice.

6 Kim Parker and Eileen Patten, "The Sandwich Generation: Rising Financial Burdens for Middle-Aged Americans," Pew Research Center, January 30, 2013, http://www.pewsocialtrends.org/2013/01/30/the-sandwich-generation/.

7 "Recognizing Caregiver Burnout," WebMD, http://www.webmd.com/women/caregiver-recognizing-burnout#1.

8 Andrew Murray, *Abide in Christ,* ReadaClassic.com, 2010, 71.

9 Romeo Vitelli, Ph.D., "Grief, Loneliness, and Losing a Spouse," *Psychology Today*, March 16, 2015, https://www.psychologytoday.com/blog/media-spotlight/201503/grief-loneliness-and-losing-spouse.

10 Melissa Dahl, "The Science of Longtime Couples Who Die Close Together," *New York* magazine, November 19, 2015, http://nymag.com/scienceofus/2015/11/science-of-longtime-couples-who-die-together.html.

Chapter 7

1 Julie Axelrod, "The Five Stages of Grief and Loss," PsychCentral, https://psychcentral.com/lib/the-5-stages-of-loss-and-grief/.

2 Nara Schoenberg, "How to Help a Child Overcome the Worst Nightmare: Death of a Parent," *Chicago Tribune*, December 23, 2014, http://www.chicagotribune.com/lifestyles/health/sc-health-1224-when-parents-die-20141218-story.html.

3 Kay Tang, "The Effects on Teenagers' Self-Esteem after Losing Parents," LiveStrong, last modified June 13, 2017, http://www.livestrong.com/article/545728-the-effects-on-teenagers-self-esteem-after-losing-parents/.

4 "Death of a Parent in Childhood Associated with Increased Suicide Risk," ScienceDaily, November 11, 2015, https://www.sciencedaily.com/releases/2015/11/151111114815.htm.

5 Schoenberg, "How to Help a Child Overcome the Worst Nightmare: Death of a Parent."

6 https://kimwencl.com/2011/09/09/eight.

NOTES

NOTES

NOTES

NOTES

NOTES

NOTES

NOTES

NOTES

If you would like to read more inspiring
and encouraging stories about God's grace
through difficult circumstances, go to:

StoriesofGodsGrace.com